First World War
and Army of Occupation
War Diary
France, Belgium and Germany

19 DIVISION
Divisional Troops
Royal Army Veterinary Corps
31 Mobile Veterinary Section
19 July 1915 - 31 January 1919

WO95/2074/1

The Naval & Military Press Ltd
www.nmarchive.com
Published in association with The National Archives

Published by

The Naval & Military Press Ltd

Unit 10 Ridgewood Industrial Park,

Uckfield, East Sussex,

TN22 5QE England

Tel: +44 (0) 1825 749494

www.naval-military-press.com

www.nmarchive.com

This diary has been reprinted in facsimile from the original. Any imperfections are inevitably reproduced and the quality may fall short of modern type and cartographic standards.

© **Crown Copyright**
Images reproduced by permission of The National Archives, London, England, 2015.

Contents

Document type	Place/Title	Date From	Date To
Heading	WO95/2074/1 19 Divn 30 Mobile Vet. Section 1915 July-1919 Jan		
Heading	31st Mob. Vety Service Jly 1915-Jan 1919		
Heading	19th Division 31st M. V. S. Vol. I		
War Diary	Southampton	19/07/1915	19/07/1915
War Diary	Le Havre	20/07/1915	21/07/1915
War Diary	St Omer	22/07/1915	22/07/1915
War Diary	Tilques	23/07/1915	23/07/1915
War Diary	Lynde	24/07/1915	24/07/1915
War Diary	St. Hilaires	25/07/1915	25/07/1915
War Diary	Busnes	26/07/1915	31/07/1915
Heading	19th Division 31st Mobile Vet Set Vol I		
War Diary	Merville	01/08/1915	31/08/1915
Heading	19th Division 31st Mobile Vet: Sect. Vol II Sept 15		
War Diary	Locon	01/09/1915	30/09/1915
Heading	19th Division 31st Mobile Vet. Sect. Vol 3 Oct 15		
War Diary	Locon	01/10/1915	03/10/1915
War Diary	Paradis	04/10/1915	20/10/1915
War Diary	Locon	21/10/1915	31/10/1915
Heading	19th Division 31st Mobile Vet Sect. Vol 4 Nov 15		
War Diary	Locon	01/11/1915	24/11/1915
War Diary	St. Venant	25/11/1915	30/11/1915
Heading	19th Division 31st Mob Vet. Sect. Vol 5 Dec 15		
War Diary	St Venant	01/12/1915	05/12/1915
War Diary	Paradis	06/12/1915	31/12/1915
Heading	19th Div 31st Mob Vet. Sect. Vol 6		
War Diary	Paradis	01/01/1916	27/01/1916
War Diary	St Venant	28/01/1916	31/01/1916
Heading	19 31st Mob Vet. Sect. Vol 7		
War Diary	St. Venant	01/02/1916	19/02/1916
War Diary	Lagorgue	20/02/1916	29/02/1916
War Diary	La Gorgue	01/03/1916	17/04/1916
War Diary	St. Venant	18/04/1916	21/04/1916
War Diary	St Hilaire	22/04/1916	30/04/1916
War Diary	St Hilaire	01/05/1916	09/05/1916
War Diary	Longheau	10/05/1916	10/05/1916
War Diary	St Vast	11/05/1916	16/06/1916
War Diary	Frechencourt	17/06/1916	30/07/1916
War Diary	Lavieville	01/07/1916	22/07/1916
War Diary	Albert	23/07/1916	24/07/1916
War Diary	Lavieville	25/07/1916	02/08/1916
War Diary	Frechencourt	03/08/1916	03/08/1916
War Diary	Long	04/08/1916	07/08/1916
War Diary	Westoutre	08/08/1916	06/09/1916
War Diary	Nieppe	07/09/1916	02/10/1916
War Diary	Vieux-Berquin	03/10/1916	06/10/1916
War Diary	Authie	07/10/1916	17/10/1916
War Diary	Contay	18/10/1916	21/10/1916
War Diary	Bouzincourt	22/10/1916	31/10/1916
Heading	M. V. S.		

War Diary	Bouzincourt	01/11/1916	24/11/1916
War Diary	Bernaville	25/11/1916	09/01/1917
War Diary	Authie	10/01/1917	21/02/1917
War Diary	Bus. Les. Artois	22/02/1917	10/03/1917
War Diary	Occoches	11/03/1917	11/03/1917
War Diary	Monchel	12/03/1917	12/03/1917
War Diary	Maegingheun	13/03/1917	14/03/1917
War Diary	Helaire-Cothes	15/03/1917	16/03/1917
War Diary	Steeubecque	17/03/1917	17/03/1917
War Diary	Lieuf. Berquin Fletre	19/03/1917	30/03/1917
War Diary	Westoutre	31/03/1917	01/05/1917
War Diary	Poperinghe	02/05/1917	10/05/1917
War Diary	Westoutre	11/05/1917	14/06/1917
War Diary	Locre	15/06/1917	19/06/1917
War Diary	St Jans Capel	20/06/1917	01/07/1917
War Diary	Lacre	03/07/1917	07/08/1917
War Diary	St Jans Capel	08/08/1917	08/08/1917
War Diary	Watton Capel	09/08/1917	09/08/1917
War Diary	Arques	10/08/1917	10/08/1917
War Diary	Mielles Lez Blequin	11/08/1917	26/08/1917
War Diary	Arques	27/08/1917	27/08/1917
War Diary	Staple	28/08/1917	28/08/1917
War Diary	St Jans Capel	29/08/1917	09/09/1917
War Diary	Locre	10/09/1917	10/11/1917
War Diary	Merris	11/11/1917	12/11/1917
War Diary	Racquinhem	13/11/1917	30/11/1917
War Diary	Field Racquinghem	01/12/1917	08/12/1917
War Diary	Achiet. Le Petit O.36. C.57	09/12/1917	12/12/1917
War Diary	036 65.7 Field	13/12/1917	13/12/1917
War Diary	Manancourt	14/12/1917	15/12/1917
War Diary	Neuville	16/12/1917	26/12/1917
War Diary	Field Neuville	27/12/1917	31/12/1917
War Diary	Neuville	01/01/1918	14/02/1918
War Diary	Le Mesnil	15/02/1918	23/03/1918
War Diary	Bucquoy	24/03/1918	24/03/1918
War Diary	Henu	25/03/1918	25/03/1918
War Diary	Mondicourt	26/03/1918	30/03/1918
War Diary	Dranoutre	31/03/1918	02/04/1918
War Diary	Nieppe	03/04/1918	10/04/1918
War Diary	Croix De Poperinghe	11/04/1918	12/04/1918
War Diary	Boeschepe	12/04/1918	12/04/1918
War Diary	L 29. A. Central	13/04/1918	16/04/1918
War Diary	Abeele	17/04/1918	20/04/1918
War Diary	Proven	21/04/1918	22/04/1918
War Diary	Godewaersvelde	23/04/1918	04/05/1918
War Diary	K 30. A. 6. 6. Sheet 24	05/05/1918	17/05/1918
War Diary	On Train	18/05/1918	18/05/1918
War Diary	Chepy	19/05/1918	28/05/1918
War Diary	Aigny	29/05/1918	29/05/1918
War Diary	Ventreuil	30/05/1918	30/05/1918
War Diary	Maufaux	31/05/1918	31/05/1918
War Diary	Nanteuil	01/06/1918	02/06/1918
War Diary	Pierry	03/06/1918	20/06/1918
War Diary	Le Mesnil Sun Oger	21/06/1918	21/06/1918
War Diary	Reuves	22/06/1918	25/06/1918
War Diary	Bannes	26/06/1918	01/07/1918

War Diary	Fere-Champenoise	02/07/1918	02/07/1918
War Diary	Maresquel	03/07/1918	03/07/1918
War Diary	Bourthes	04/07/1918	07/07/1918
War Diary	Mill S. Of Bout-De-La-Ville	08/07/1918	13/07/1918
War Diary	Bellery	14/07/1918	06/08/1918
War Diary	Lapognoy (D19. D 9, 5 Sheet 445)	07/08/1918	07/08/1918
War Diary	Bois-Des Dames	08/08/1918	24/08/1918
War Diary	Lapognoy	25/08/1918	31/08/1918
War Diary	Lapugnoy D19. D. 95. (Sheet 445)	01/09/1918	03/09/1918
War Diary	Le Hamel (V. 22.a 4.5) (Sheet 36a)	04/09/1918	17/09/1918
War Diary	Belzage Farm. (W. 22 D. B8) (Sheet 36.a)	18/09/1918	01/10/1918
War Diary	Pernes	02/10/1918	04/10/1918
War Diary	Givenchy Le-Noble	05/10/1918	05/10/1918
War Diary	Sombrin	06/10/1918	06/10/1918
War Diary	Boisleux	07/10/1918	07/10/1918
War Diary	Between Graincourt & Canal Du Nord	08/10/1918	08/10/1918
War Diary	Between Graincourt & Canal Du Nord	09/10/1918	09/10/1918
War Diary	Between Graincourt & Canal Du Nord	10/10/1918	10/10/1918
War Diary	Novelles Sur L'escaut	11/10/1918	14/10/1918
War Diary	Cambrai A. 53. B. 9.1	15/10/1918	18/10/1918
War Diary	C. 4 B. 5.9 Sheet 57.b	19/10/1918	23/10/1918
War Diary	Rieux	24/10/1918	03/11/1918
War Diary	St. Albert	04/11/1918	04/11/1918
War Diary	Vendegies	05/11/1918	05/11/1918
War Diary	Sepmeries	06/11/1918	06/11/1918
War Diary	Jenlain	07/11/1918	08/11/1918
War Diary	Flamengries	09/11/1918	10/11/1918
War Diary	Bry	11/11/1918	14/11/1918
War Diary	Vendegies	15/11/1918	15/11/1918
War Diary	Rieux	16/11/1918	25/11/1918
War Diary	Cambrai	26/11/1918	26/11/1918
War Diary	Butte De Warlencourt	27/11/1918	27/11/1918
War Diary	Candas	28/11/1918	30/11/1918
War Diary	Montrelet	01/01/1919	31/01/1919

WO 95 2074/1

19 Divn.
31 Mobile Vet. Section
1915 JULY - 1919 FEB JAN

WAS 2074 JAN

19TH DIVISION

31ST MOB. VETY SERVICE

JLY 1915 - JAN 1919

19th Division

31st M.V.S.
Headquarters 19th Division
A.D.V.S.
Vol. I

12/6357

Brid

L

January 1915
Jan '15

Army Form C. 2118.

WAR DIARY
or
INTELLIGENCE SUMMARY.
(Erase heading not required.)

31st Mobile Veterinary Section
19th Division

Instructions regarding War Diaries and Intelligence Summaries are contained in F. S. Regs., Part II. and the Staff Manual respectively. Title pages will be prepared in manuscript.

Place	Date	Hour	Summary of Events and Information	Remarks and references to Appendices
SOUTHAMPTON	19/7/15	2 P.m.	Embarked with Mobile Section.	
LE HAVRE	20/7/15	7 a.m.	Disembarked Section marched to No 5 Rest-Camp after drawing remainder of equipment from Wharf.	
LE HAVRE	21/7/15	7 a.m.	Entrained	
ST. OMER	22/7/15	7 a.m.	Disentrained. Section marched to Billets at TILQUES about three miles out. Billets satisfactory. Men under cover. Horses picketed in field adjoining near Billet. Information received from O.C. 81 Field.Coy R.E. that a lame horse would be unable to proceed with rest the following morning. An N.C.O. and Pte. proceeded to R.E Billet at Sercques and brought horse to the Section the following morning. Information received from 20 I/c 88th & 89th Bdes of horses left at TOURNEHEM and BONNINGUES also from G.O.C. 57th Inf. Bde. of one horse left at NIELLES LEZ ARDRES. The nearest Vet. office 20.1/c Vet Hospital St. Omer was informed for necessary action.	
TILQUES	23/7/15	9.45 a.m.	One N.C.O. proceeded to Vet Hosp. ST OMER to hand over two sick horses of the 36th Inf Bde unable to accompany the Section. Section marched to Lynde about three miles. Roads good. Weather changeable. Billets satisfactory. Men under cover. Horses in open.	
LYNDE	24/7/15	9.30 a.m.	Section marched to ST. HILAIRES about 12 miles. Roads good. Weather fine Billets excellent. Room for horses and men under cover.	
ST. HILAIRES	25/7/15	3 P.m.	Section marched to Desvres about 6 miles. Roads good. Weather fine	

Army Form C. 2118.

WAR DIARY
or
INTELLIGENCE SUMMARY. 31st Mobile Veterinary Section
(Erase heading not required.)

19th Division

Instructions regarding War Diaries and Intelligence Summaries are contained in F.S. Regs., Part II. and the Staff Manual respectively. Title pages will be prepared in manuscript.

Place	Date	Hour	Summary of Events and Information	Remarks and references to Appendices
BUSNES	26/7/15		Billets satisfactory. Horses picketed in a field. Men under canvas adjoining.	
"	27/7/15		Visited LYNDE and RENESCURE, southern sections. Watered and hours left behind by units. Horse at Renescure unable to march. Informed A.D.V.S. for necessary action.	
	30/7/15		Visited horse at ISBERGUES about five miles left behind by Nyoratus 57th Inf Bde. Destroyed horse on account of Rinderpest. Entrained fourteen horses at LILLERS for No 5 Vet Hospital Abbeville. Sent N.C.O. and one man to collect horses from 88th Bde. R.F.A. at BOURECQ about three miles.	
	31/7/15		Transferred three horses (one by hand [faint]) to No 12 Mob. Vet Section & 4th Division at LILLERS for entrainment to Vet Hospital Abbeville.	
		2 pm	Section marched to Merville. Billets satisfactory. Remarks good. Westhorpe. Dummy picnic clean duty. Three horses have been evacuated by the Section, of which	
			1 & had been sent to No 5 Para. Hospital Abbeville	
			2 to Vet Hospital St Omer	
			3 to No 12 Mobile Vet Section for entrainment to Base	
			4 Cases and returned to Units	
			20 Remain with Section for treatment	

MERVILLE 31/7/15

N. Somerhaye
Capt
O.C

12/6694

19th Division

31st mobile vet: sect:
Vol: I

July & August/15

WAR DIARY or INTELLIGENCE SUMMARY

Army Form C. 2118

31st Mobile Vet. Section

Place	Date	Hour	Summary of Events and Information	Remarks and references to Appendices
MERVILLE	1/8/15	—	Billet consisted of a room for the men and his small adjoining field for the horses. Walls softly constructed and convenient. Billet being on the side of a canal. There were a number of small open sheds which were used for harness, it was also possible to hack under eaves, a phenomenon and a mess for the men. The sick horses were picketed in one field and another section lines in the other. Twenty two horses were necessary under treatment, six of which were admitted to hospital. Routine work. Weather favourable. Method of picketing – Head line for each horse, ground line, heel ropes for hind legs.	
	2/8/15		10 horses admitted, one died and one cured, 2 ; 2 convoy runs linked	
	3/8/15		3 horses admitted and 2 returned to work for duty	
	4/8/15		1 horse admitted	
	5/8/15		7 horses admitted and 2 returned to work for duty	
	6/8/15		2 horses admitted, 12 horses transferred to Base Hospital ABBEVILLE accompanied by a Corporal and his men	
	7/8/15		3 horses admitted and 1 died. Conducting party returned	
	8/8/15		4 horses admitted	
	9/8/15		3 horses admitted. Telephone and lucilerent to Liverp. for staff.	
	10/8/15		3 horses admitted, 1 died and 3 discharged to Unit for duty	
	11/8/15		1 horse admitted and 1 returned to work for duty	
	12/8/15		8 horses admitted, 16 horses entrained for Hospital ABBEVILLE with conducting party consisting of 1 NCO and three men	
	13/8/15		Conducting party returned. 1 private is sent to the BASE sick and struck off the strength of the section.	
	14/8/15		2 horses admitted and 1 Discharged to Unit for duty	
	15/8/15		5 horses admitted	
	16/8/15		7 horses admitted and 1 discharged to Unit for duty. 1 Sergeant returns to section for duty and is taken on the strength	
	17/8/15		3 horses admitted, 2 Discharged to Unit for duty. 17 Transferred by rail to Hospital ABBEVILLE with usual Conducting party	
	18/8/15		1 horse admitted, 4 Discharged to Unit for duty. Return of conducting party	
	19/8/15		3 horses admitted	
	20/8/15		1 horse admitted 4 Discharged to Unit for duty	

Army Form C. 2118.

WAR DIARY
or
INTELLIGENCE SUMMARY.
(Erase heading not required.)

31st Mobile V.S. Section

Instructions regarding War Diaries and Intelligence Summaries are contained in F. S. Regs., Part II. and the Staff Manual respectively. Title pages will be prepared in manuscript.

Hour, Date, Place	Summary of Events and Information	Remarks and References to Appendices
MERVILLE 21/8/15	Routine Work. 2 horses admitted. 1 Discharged incurable. D.D.V.S. interview. O.V.C. N.C.O. attached to 31st Mobile Veterinary Section.	
22/8/15	Routine Work. 1 Horse admitted. 1 Discharged to Unit for duty.	
23/8/15	Two mares sent Michelez sick, weak. Routine Work. 8 Horses admitted. 1 Discharged to Unit for duty.	
24/8/15	Routine Work. 2 horses inspected. Army Vet. Inspector inspected for gun horses lame and projected by means of flag and head collar also to be secured by a Neil saddle. Two horses not of weight enough and lame [?] went out of hand after which I carried out by P.S. note became lame. Limited the meaning of the horse entering by Neil saddle moved the flag.	
25/8/15	Routine Work. 1 horse admitted. 1 Discharged to Unit for duty.	
26/8/15	Routine Work. 4 Horses admitted. 2 Retained. 1 sent for duty accompanied by NCO.	
27/8/15	117 inspected & made for Public attention accompanied by NCO and 9th man. Routine Work. 2 Horses admitted. 2 Discharged to unit for duty.	
28/8/15	Routine Work. 1 mule & 1 horse admitted. 1 sent to Abbeville.	
29/8/15	Routine Work. Two horses admitted. 1 Brought in horse from last	
30/8/15	Routine Work. 1 NCO and 1 horse with urgent message to LOCON	
31/8/15	5 Letters and 1 new boot box from 1/2 Mobile Veterinary Section. Removed of ration forward by road to LOCON where we order	

121/6991

19th Kurann

31st Mobile Vet. Sect.

Vol II

Sept. 15

ard

Army Form C. 2118.

WAR DIARY
or
INTELLIGENCE SUMMARY. 31st Mobile Section

(Erase heading not required.)

Instructions regarding War Diaries and Intelligence Summaries are contained in F. S. Regs., Part II. and the Staff Manual respectively. Title pages will be prepared in manuscript.

Hour, Date, Place	Summary of Events and Information	Remarks and References to Appendices
1/9/15 LOCON	Reletments of this returns and a puddock adjoining, a barn and two wagon sheds partially occupied. Such rebuilt offrots transferred were for left section horses and such and will be occupied directly as the condition of the standing necessitate. The puddock will be used for exercise lines. One shed counted as a line for equipment and shoeing, the other will be used for wagons in any such cases that might arise. An portably loan useful in eventual and ground has first down in the paddock Road that for reconnelling find, started at CHOQUES between fine and six miles away by road whilst at excess No 6574 Pt Munell was thrown from his horse and received severe injuries nonothelise his internal state remained of report Routine Work	
2/9/15	" Death of No 6574 Pt Munell admitted from hospital	
3/9/15	"	
4/9/15	"	
5/9/15	"	
6/9/15	"	
7/9/15	"	
8/9/15	"	
9/9/15	16 Horses and two 2 mules responded to Divn Mobile ABBEVILLE accompanied by mounted orderly party for way lire are returned by flood which was lived from a tender at BETHUNE. A horse & mule floot was lived from the Divisional Train.	
10/9/15	Routine Work Responded 13 horses and 9 mules to ABBEVILLE	
11/9/15	No 1410 Pt Redford started from no 9 Red Hospital Doulla BOULOGNE	
12/9/15	and to return in the Hospital	

Army Form C. 2118.

WAR DIARY
or
INTELLIGENCE SUMMARY.
(Erase heading not required.)

31st Mobile Vet Section (Units)

Instructions regarding War Diaries and Intelligence Summaries are contained in F. S. Regs., Part II. and the Staff Manual respectively. Title pages will be prepared in manuscript.

Hour, Date, Place	Summary of Events and Information	Remarks and References to Appendices
12/9/15 LOCON	10 Horses and 2 mules evacuated to ABBEVILLE. 7 Cast hand & convoy of 2 horses to Raw Head	
13/9/15 "	8 Horses and evacuated to ABBEVILLE. 7 Cast hand & convoy two horses to Raw Head	
14/9/15 "	Routine Work	
15/9/15 "	Evacuated to ABBEVILLE 9 horses & 3 mules	
16/9/15 "	" " 2 " 4 4 " 7 Cast hand	
17/9/15 "	1 convoy one horse and one mule.	
18/9/15 "	Routine Work	
19/9/15 "	" "	
20/9/15 "	Horse Transport Driver ABBEVILLE and was transferred to B. V. & S. Wagon reported at LEFACON about his mules from own Section	
21/9/15 "	Routine Work	
22/9/15 "	Advance Dressing Post consisting of 1 NCO and 3 men joined at LEFACON. Evacuated 13 horses and 2 mules to hres ABBEVILLE	
23/9/15 "	Routine Work	
24/9/15 "	3 Mules suffering from Broad regimen evacuated to ABBEVILLE. 7 Cast hand & convoy	
25/9/15 "	Evacuated 20 horses & 3 mules to ABBEVILLE. 7 Cast hand & convoy 1 horse from that to Vitrin Manor to Raw Head and late to collect one horse from unit at LEGLATIGNIES & convey to Section	
26/9/15 "	Routine Work	
27/9/15 "	" "	

Army Form C. 2118.

WAR DIARY
or
INTELLIGENCE SUMMARY. 31st Mobile Veterinary Section (contd)
(Erase heading not required.)

Hour, Date, Place	Summary of Events and Information	Remarks and References to Appendices
28/9/15 LOCON	Routine Work. Advance Dressing Post brought in	
29/9/15 "	Evacuated 13 horses and 3 mules. 3 mules to ABBEVILLE # Cont'd horse & convoy horse & Remit Headqrs. Standing of Horse Lines very slack owing to heavy rain.	
30/9/15 "	Routine Work.	

Army Form C. 2118.

WAR DIARY
or
INTELLIGENCE SUMMARY.
(Erase heading not required.) 3/2 Norfolk Section

Instructions regarding War Diaries and Intelligence Summaries are contained in F. S. Regs., Part II. and the Staff Manual respectively. Title pages will be prepared in manuscript.

Hour, Date, Place	Summary of Events and Information	Remarks and References to Appendices
1/9/15 LOCON	Relief movement of horse standards and a practical refreshers in Camp and two wagons fitted for ambulance work. Pack mules & carts & influenza for left section horses and such and will be carefully observed as to conditions of the standing vaccination. The wounded will need further inoculation. Horses when hit by shell, invalided mules or slain or employed out and showing the effect will be used for organising and sent Next runnings of influenza. The two officers left for the men in the fatigues. Some wounded in returns and ground had fell down in the high. Red Shed has remaining Right situated at ETOCQUES between four and six horses away by mind & and several was in reserve. No 5 SN + 6h trained man horses lost some What it ensures and several sewer injures necessitating his immediate removal to hospital.	
2/9/15	Routine work	
3/9/15	"	
4/9/15	"	
5/9/15	"	Death of No 6372 Pte Maxwell who died from hospital
6/9/15	"	
7/9/15	"	
8/9/15	"	
9/9/15	"4 horses and two 2 mules evacuated to Base Kennels ABBEVILLE accompanied by mount conducting party by my bus. was covered 7 Refrit which was brought from a number of BETHUNE. A lens army Post area had from the Divisional Front.	
10/9/15	Section Orders Issued by 13 horses and 2 mules - ABBEVILLE	
11/9/15	2 mules Ordered to Stationary L.P. Vet Hospital Bologne BOULOGNE	
12/9/15		

Army Form C. 2118.

WAR DIARY
or
INTELLIGENCE SUMMARY.
(Erase heading not required.)

31st Mobile Vet. Section (Units)

Instructions regarding War Diaries and Intelligence Summaries are contained in F. S. Regs., Part II. and the Staff Manual respectively. Title pages will be prepared in manuscript.

Hour, Date, Place	Summary of Events and Information	Remarks and References to Appendices
12/9/15 LOODH	10 Horses and 2 mules evacuated to ABBEVILLE. 7 Cart Mules & horses & 2 horses to Rail Head	
13/9/15	8 Horses evacuated to ABBEVILLE. 7 Cart Mules & horses, two horses to Rail Head	
14/9/15	Routine Work	
15/9/15	Evacuated to ABBEVILLE 2 horses & 3 mules	
16/9/15	" " 2 " & 4 " 7 Cart mules	
17/9/15	6 wings one horse and one mule. Routine Work	
18/9/15	"	
19/9/15	" Dr. & C.S. Wagon reported at Section from Ordnance. Transferred Driver ABBEVILLE and one transferred to	
20/9/15	At Divisional Train Routine Work	
21/9/15	Colonne Dunning ? not working ?/ 1 NCO and 3 men joined at LEFACON about two mules from near Section evacuated 13 Horses and 2 mules to base ABBEVILLE	
22/9/15	Routine Work	
23/9/15	3 mules suffering from Point Injuries vellies by Advance Post and sent to Field Ambulance wagons	
24/9/15	Evacuated 20 horses & 3 Mules to ABBEVILLE. 7 Cart mules & horses from unit to Indian Horses to Rail Head and Vet. I Collect no? Vet. Section at LESQLATIGNIES ? mainly ? Section	
25/9/15	Routine Work	
26/9/15	Henry Quinn	
27/9/15		

Army Form C. 2118.

WAR DIARY
or
INTELLIGENCE SUMMARY. of 31st Mobile Veterinary Section (held)
(Erase heading not required.)

Instructions regarding War Diaries and Intelligence Summaries are contained in F. S. Regs., Part II. and the Staff Manual respectively. Title pages will be prepared in manuscript.

Hour, Date, Place	Summary of Events and Information	Remarks and References to Appendices
28/9/15 LOGON	Rubbit Work	
29/9/15 "	Inspected 10 horses and 3 mules at ABBEVILLE Went round & owning home to Rail Head. Standing of horselines very short owing to heavy rains. Routine Work.	W. Rose Capt. A.V.C. O.C. 31st Mobile Vet Section. F.a.s.u.
30/9/15	Routine Work.	

121/7432

19th Kurram

31st Mobile Vet. Sect.
Vol: 3

Oct 15

Army Form C. 2118.

WAR DIARY
or
INTELLIGENCE SUMMARY.
(Erase heading not required.)

Army Form C. 2118 _____ 31st Mobile Veterinary Section

Instructions regarding War Diaries and Intelligence Summaries are contained in F. S. Regs., Part II. and the Staff Manual respectively. Title pages will be prepared in manuscript.

Hour, Date, Place	Summary of Events and Information	Remarks and References to Appendices
1/10/15 LONDON	Routine Work	
2/10/15	Received orders to proceed to and proceeded to the Remount news to fit out for field	
3/10/15 11 am	Entrained & arrived LILLE at PARADIS about 11 pm	
	Horses were picketed in the orchard and reference was made to the farm which was also used for an equipment & harness store. The Officer & 6 both have accommodation in rooms at a cottage but 6 of the junior old ranks [?] have to sleep on straw under the picketing lines in the open [?]	
4/10/15 PARADIS	Routine Work	
5/10/15 "	Searched a casualty post at FOSSE about two miles away consisting of an NCO and two men. Supplemented by horse to AZEEVILLE	
6/10/15 "	Routine Work	
	Billet situated at CALONNE about two miles	
7/10/15 "	" "	
8/10/15 "	" "	
9/10/15 "	" "	
10/10/15 "	" "	

Army Form C. 2118.

WAR DIARY
or
INTELLIGENCE SUMMARY.
(Erase heading not required.)

1st Mobile Vet. Section

Instructions regarding War Diaries and Intelligence Summaries are contained in F. S. Regs., Part II. and the Staff Manual respectively. Title pages will be prepared in manuscript.

Hour, Date, Place	Summary of Events and Information	Remarks and References to Appendices
11/10/15 PARADIS	Routine Work	
12/10/15 "	Routine Work. Overnight sedick had three mules to ABBEVILLE	
13/10/15 "	ABBEVILLE. Routine Work	
14/10/15 "	"	
15/10/15 "	Evacuated one horse and two mules to Base Hospital ABBEVILLE	
16/10/15 "	Routine Work	
17/10/15 "	"	
18/10/15 "	"	
19/10/15 "	"	
20/10/15 "	2 evacuated. Indian horse and three mules	
21/10/15 LOGON	to R.V.H ABBEVILLE. Indian returned to unit. MOI left at 10.20 AM.	
22/10/15 "	Routine Work	
23/10/15 "	" horse Veterinary Officer found one dead mong to buy waggon	
24/10/15 "	" Commenced to Cap Service tests of cavalry horses	
25/10/15 "	" Evacuated one horse and two mules to ABBEVILLE	
26/10/15 "	" In accordance with Divisional Orders issued.	
27/10/15 "	Rough C.R.E. for mistreat horses to Coin to four lord horses	

Army Form C. 2118.

WAR DIARY
or
INTELLIGENCE SUMMARY. 31st Mobile Vet Section
(Erase heading not required.)

Instructions regarding War Diaries and Intelligence Summaries are contained in F. S. Regs., Part II. and the Staff Manual respectively. Title pages will be prepared in manuscript.

Hour, Date, Place	Summary of Events and Information	Remarks and References to Appendices
28/10/15 LOSON	Routine Work.	
29/10/15 "	"	
30/10/15 "	"	
31/10/15 "	"	

N.T. = no Captain O.C.
O.C. 31st Mobile Vet Section

12/7621

19th Kursun

31st Infs. Reft. Sect:
vol: 4

Nov 15

WAR DIARY or INTELLIGENCE SUMMARY

Army Form C. 2118

(Erase heading not required.)

31st Mobile Veterinary Section

Instructions regarding War Diaries and Intelligence Summaries are contained in F.S. Regs., Part II. and the Staff Manual respectively. Title Pages will be prepared in manuscript.

Place	Date	Hour	Summary of Events and Information	Remarks and references to Appendices
LOCON	1/11/15		Routine work. Commenced to Coy shown brick stainings for horses.	
"	2/11/15		Evacuated 12 horses and 6 mules to No 5 Veterinary Hospital ABBEVILLE	
"	3/11/15		Routine work. Opened up a collecting post at CORNET MALO to collect sick from units in ROBECQ AREA	ROBECQ AREA
"	4/11/15		Routine work.	
"	5/11/15		Routine work.	
"	6/11/15		Routine work.	
"	7/11/15		Evacuated six horses and his mules belonging to Mount Division and no mule mens horse of the 19th Division	
"	8/11/15		Routine work.	
"	9/11/15		Routine work.	
"	10/11/15		Evacuated fifteen horses and one mule of Mount Division and fourteen horses one mule of the 19th Division	
"	11/11/15		Routine Work.	
"	12/11/15		Evacuated six horses of the Mount Division and three horses of the 19th Division	
"	13/11/15		Routine Work	
"	14/11/15		Routine Work	
"	15/11/15		Routine Work	
"	16/11/15		Evacuated five horses and five mules. Took in veterinary charge of the 57th Infantry Bde	
"	17/11/15		Collected 1-4 horses of the Mount Division at BUSNES, amounting them to ABBEVILLE together with sick horses and foot mules of the 19th Division the same day.	
"	18/11/15		Routine Work. Two men report sick and are evacuated to LILLERS. Boy of Claunig Rattali	
"	19/11/15		Evacuated ten horses and one mule. Section billeted & billet at ST VENANT	ST VENANT
"			received orders from A.D.V.S. 19th Division	
"	20/11/15		Routine Work.	
"	21/11/15		Routine Work.	
"	22/11/15		Evacuated twenty four horses and two mules. Recalled collecting Post from CORNET MALO	CORNET MALO
"			Sent an N.C.O and one man to prepare new billet at ST VENANT for around of section

:375 Wt. W593/826 1,000,000 4/15 J.R.C. & A. A.D.S.S./Forms/C.2118.

WAR DIARY
or
INTELLIGENCE SUMMARY 31st Mobile Veterinary Section

Army Form C. 2118

Place	Date	Hour	Summary of Events and Information	Remarks and references to Appendices
LOCON	23/11/15		Routine Work. One mare returned from hospital LILLERS. Hired a horse float from MERVILLE for conveyance of horses unable to walk.	
"	24/11/15		Proceeded to horse billet at ST VENANT, leaving one N.C.O. and three men at LOCON as a collecting post for units of the Division remaining in that area. Invaluated five mules.	
ST VENANT	25/11/15		Billet consists of a large gateway, affording room in wagon shed etc. but few of the section hitherto. Accommodation for none of the section sufficient. Invaluated 2 horses by float from LOCON.	
"	26/11/15		Invaluated some horses and his mules from ST VENANT, CALONNE. Started about three mules away being (the Rd Head.	
"	27/11/15		Routine Work. Hundred and fifty-seven (157) # 9 of Rifle to cond the V.O. commenced to lay down brick standings for horses.	
"	28/11/15		Invaluated twelve horses and one mule (veterinary case) and fourteen horses, two mules (Remount Cases) to ABBEVILLE.	
"	29/11/15		Routine Work. Invalided for Material L, invest stable for twenty horses.	
"	30/11/15		Routine Work.	
			During the month the weather has been changeable, rendering it very trying to horses not provided with brick standings or shelter. General health of the section has been satisfactory.	

N.T. ...... Capt. A.V.C.
O.C. 31st M.V.S.

31st October, deer.
Vol: 5

19th November

121/7795

Dec 15

a v o

WAR DIARY
or
INTELLIGENCE SUMMARY

Army Form C. 2118

(Erase heading not required.)

3/1st Suffolk Yeomanry Section

Instructions regarding War Diaries and Intelligence Summaries are contained in F.S. Regs., Part II. and the Staff Manual respectively. Title Pages will be prepared in manuscript.

Place	Date	Hour	Summary of Events and Information	Remarks and references to Appendices
ST. VENANT	1/12/15		Evacuated 14 horses. Routine work	
"	2/12/15		Evacuated 9 horses and two mules	
"	3/12/15		Evacuated 12 horses	
"	4/12/15			
"	5/12/15		Proceeded to new billet at PARADIS. Visited CROIX MARRAISE. Collect horse left behind by D.A.C. Routine work. Visited Quante Divisional Train to collect horse of 19th D.A.C. having front of turn. also visited VIER-HOUCK to collect horse of Lyd North Soties.	
PARADIS	6/12/15		Routine Work. One Pte joined section from No 3 Mobile PONT du BRICQUE. Collect PONT RIQUEUL horse left behind by 46th Division. Visited Collecting Station at LA FOSSE and LOCON	
"	7/12/15			
"	8/12/15		Evacuated five mules and seven horses.	
"	9/12/15		Hind foot for conveyance of sick horse from PONT RIQUEUL to section. Also collected horse of 46th Division at VIEILLE DE CHAPELLE. Sent an N.C.O. to disinfect a stable at LESTREM reported to have been inserted by a horse with Contagious Disease.	
"	10/12/15		Routine Work. Visited LACOUTURE and VIEILLE CHAPELLE to collect horses left behind by 46th Division.	
"	11/12/15		Evacuated 21 horses and three mules. All horses of section tested with Mallein	
"	12/12/15		Collected horses from LESTREM and PONT RIQUEUL. Routine Work	
"	13/12/15		Routine Work	
"	14/12/15		Routine Work	
"	15/12/15		Evacuated 21 horses & 2 mules	
"	16/12/15		Drew wood from FORET de NIEPPE for erecting wind screen to standings Routine Work	
"	17/12/15		" "	
"	18/12/15		Evacuated 2.5 horses and three mules. Routine Work. Put down a brush planting for isolation area.	
"	19/12/15		" "	
"	20/12/15		" "	
"	21/12/15			
"	22/12/15			
"	23/12/15		Evacuated 21 horses and 4 mules. Routine Work. Wind Flint for horse of J.G Battery R.H.A. 38 to D.h.	
"	24/12/15			
"	25/12/15			

Army Form C. 2118

WAR DIARY
or
INTELLIGENCE SUMMARY

(Erase heading not required.) 31st Mobile Veterinary Section

Instructions regarding War Diaries and Intelligence Summaries are contained in F.S. Regs., Part II. and the Staff Manual respectively. Title Pages will be prepared in manuscript.

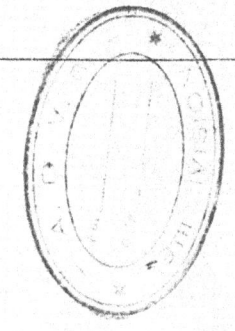

Place	Date	Hour	Summary of Events and Information	Remarks and references to Appendices
PARADIS	26/12/15		Routine Work. Assisted in the mustering of horses of the Yorkshire Dragoons.	
"	27/12/15		" " kind fleet for horses of 66th & 99th Bde R.F.A. Assisted in the mustering of horses of the 38th & 7th Field Ambulance & a Section of F.A.C.	
"	28/12/15		Routine Work. Kind.	
"	29/12/15		Routine Work. Mustered horses of the 59th Field Ambulance.	
"	30/12/15		Windflint to remove horse from collecting station at LOCON. Routine work.	
"	31/12/15		Routine work.	

N.T. me Cutt a.v.c.
O.C. 31st M.V.S.

31st Indn: Vet: Sect:
Vol: 6

19th Div.

Army Form C. 2118

WAR DIARY or INTELLIGENCE SUMMARY

31st Mobile Veterinary Section

(Erase heading not required.)

Place	Date	Hour	Summary of Events and Information	Remarks and references to Appendices
PARADIS	1/1/16		Evacuated 28 horses to ABBEVILLE.	
"	2/1/16		Routine Work. Collected horse by float from J. Battery R.H.A.	
"	3/1/16		Evacuated 14 horses to ABBEVILLE, three of which were taken to Railhead by float. Pulled a Section of horses of the D.A.C.	
"	4/1/16		Routine Work. Collected horses by float from "B" Battery, 88th Bde. & "J" Battery R.H.A.	
"	5/1/16		Evacuated 11 horses and 1 mule to ABBEVILLE, two horses being taken to Railhead by float.	
"	6/1/16		Routine Work.	
"	7/1/16		Evacuated 26 horses to ABBEVILLE.	
"	8/1/16		Routine Work. Arranged for float to be returned at intervals through the day. Sent a N.C.O. to see a horse left at a farm by the 2nd Cav. D.A.C.	
"	9/1/16		Routine Work.	
"	10/1/16		Routine Work. Handed our Veterinary Charge of "C" By Yorkshire Dragoons 9 & 88 #7 Field Ambulance	
"	11/1/16		Evacuated 34 horses & 1 mule to ABBEVILLE. Sergeant Eggleton Revd. (No.9362) rejoined from No 2 Vet. Hospital.	
"	12/1/16		Routine Work. 1 N.C.O. sent to Rouen for Dental Treatment	
"	13/1/16		Routine Work. Interpreter transferred to 38th Infantry Bde, the services of interpreter is still being required when required.	
"	14/1/16		Routine Work.	
"	15/1/16		Evacuated 35 horses to # & 2 mules to NEUFCHATEL.	
"	16/1/16		Routine Work.	
"	17/1/16		Evacuated 19 horses and two mules to NEUFCHATEL. Collected horses by float from 2nd London Heavy Bty, and advance collecting post at LOCON.	
"	18/1/16		Routine Work. Sergeant Eggleton R.A.V.C. transferred to No 1 Section Guards D.A.C. Collect horses by float from 112th London Heavy Battery and 82nd Bty R.E.	
"	19/1/16		Routine Work. Collected horse by float from 35th ½ Heavy Battery	

Army Form C. 2118

WAR DIARY
or
INTELLIGENCE SUMMARY   31st Mobile Veterinary Section

(Erase heading not required.)

Instructions regarding War Diaries and Intelligence Summaries are contained in F.S. Regs., Part II. and the Staff Manual respectively. Title Pages will be prepared in manuscript.

Place	Date	Hour	Summary of Events and Information	Remarks and references to Appendices
PARADIS	20/1/16		Routine Work. Collected horse by flood from 2nd London Heavy Battery.	
"	21/1/16		Evacuated 28 horses to NEUFCHATEL vary front by railway. His horse to Rail Head D.D.V.S. 1st Army visited section & inspected his horses undergoing mallein test. Had prisoners given doubtful readings.	
"	22/1/16		Routine Work. Collected horse by flood from advance post at LOCON.	
"	23/1/16		Routine Work.	
"	24/1/16		Evacuated 31 horses to NEUFCHATEL vary front to convey his horses to Rail Head & his men under N.C.O. with G.S. Limbered Wagon to AUCHY AUBOIS to report to O.C. 47 and Mobile Vet. Section. En route for ABBEVILLE to receive a Tent.	
"	25/1/16		Routine Work. Proceeded to ST. VENANT to obtain particulars of billet to be taken over from 49th M.V.S. 38th Division.	
"	26/1/16		Evacuated 38 horses to ABBEVILLE, using flood for his horses.	
"	27/1/16		Marched to new billet at ST. VENANT.	
ST VENANT	28/1/16		Billet consist of three farms, all horses and dressing hut where also taken one mile out ST. FLORIS all sick horse being transferred to this post (which one is on the way to rail head) from his ammunition. Routine Work.	
"	29/1/16		Horse collected by flood from D'Battery 122 Bd. R.F.A. 36th Division.	
"	30/1/16		Evacuated 17 horses and 4 mules to ABBEVILLE. Tent and two men arrived from ABBEVILLE.	
"	31/1/16		In the whole the wealths has been favourable. General health of men of section good.	N.T.B no Batt. U.C. O.C. 31st M.V.S

19
31st Mob: Vet: Sect:
Vol: 7

Army Form C. 2118

WAR DIARY
or
INTELLIGENCE SUMMARY

31st Mobile Veterinary Section

(Erase heading not required.)

Instructions regarding War Diaries and Intelligence Summaries are contained in F.S. Regs., Part II. and the Staff Manual respectively. Title Pages will be prepared in manuscript.

Place	Date	Hour	Summary of Events and Information	Remarks and references to Appendices
ST. VENANT	1/2/16		Routine Work. Sent a two left. By 12/ Div. A.C. 38th Divison in LE SERT. Collected two horses from F.G. troops admitted at HAVERSKERQUE.	
"	2/2/16		Routine Work	
"	3/2/16		Evacuated to NEUFCHATEL 26 horses and one mule.	
"	4/2/16		Routine Work	
"	5/2/16		" "	
"	6/2/16		Evacuated to NEUFCHATEL thirty four horses.	
"	7/2/16		Routine Work	
"	8/2/16		" "	
"	9/2/16		" " In 6443 9th F. admitted to 57th Field Ambulance as would of own accident.	
"	10/2/16		" "	
"	11/2/16		" "	
"	12/2/16		" "	
"	13/2/16		Evacuated 27 horses to NEUFCHATEL	
"	14/2/16		Routine Work	
"	15/2/16		" "	
"	16/2/16		" "	
"	17/2/16		Evacuated 19 horses and 5 mules to NEUFCHATEL	
"	18/2/16		Sent one N.C.O. to LAGORGUE to take over billet from 4.5. M.V.S. Guards Division. 7 new horses evacuated to NEUFCHATEL in anticipating of a move to new billets	
"	19/2/16		Section marched to new billet at LAGORGUE — about five miles.	

:375 Wt. W593/826 1,000,000 4/15 J.B.C. & A.   A.D.S.S./Forms/C. 2118.

Army Form C. 2118

WAR DIARY
or
INTELLIGENCE SUMMARY   31st Mobile Veterinary Section
(Erase heading not required.)

Place	Date	Hour	Summary of Events and Information	Remarks and references to Appendices
LA GORGUE	20/2/16		Horse billet used for accommodating both sick and staff horses. These are mostly sufficient stable room for any strength sick horses requiring shelter. Mon field is adjacent house.	
"	21/2/16		Routine work.	
"	22/2/16		Evacuated ~19 horses and 2 miles to NEUF CHATEL	
"	23/2/16		Routine work	
"	24/2/16		" "	
"	25/2/16		" "	
"	26/2/16		Evacuated 19 horses and 1 mule to ABBEVILLE	
"	27/2/16		Routine work	
"	28/2/16		" "	
"	29/2/16		Weather during the month has been changeable, but on the whole favourable for horses.	

N. Dunn Capt. A.V.C.
O.C. 31st M.V.S.

WAR DIARY or INTELLIGENCE SUMMARY

Army Form C. 2118

31st Mobile Veterinary Section

Place	Date	Hour	Summary of Events and Information	Remarks and references to Appendices
LA GORGUE	1/3/16	—	Evacuated 21 horses and 5 mules to the 13 Vet Hospital NEUFCHATEL	
"	2/3/16		Routine Work	
"	3/3/16		" "	
"	4/3/16		Evacuated to NEUFCHATEL 11 horses and 3 mules	
"	5/3/16		Routine Work	
"	6/3/16		" "	
"	7/3/16		Evacuated to NEUFCHATEL 15 horses and 2 mules	
"	8/3/16		Routine Work	
"	9/3/16		" "	
"	10/3/16		" "	
"	11/3/16		Evacuated 22 horses to NEUFCHATEL	
"	12/3/16		Routine Work	
"	13/3/16		" "	
"	14/3/16		" "	
"	15/3/16		25 horses evacuated to NEUFCHATEL	
"	16/3/16		Routine Work	
"	17/3/16		21 horses evacuated to NEUFCHATEL	
"	18/3/16		Routine Work	
"	19/3/16		" "	
"	20/3/16		Evacuated 22 horses and 3 mules to NEUFCHATEL. 2 men joined Section from No 6 Vet Hospital to take the place of 2 Drivers R.F.A. who had been acting as Orderlies.	

Army Form C. 2118

WAR DIARY
or
INTELLIGENCE SUMMARY   31st Mobile Veterinary Section

(Erase heading not required.)

Instructions regarding War Diaries and Intelligence Summaries are contained in F. S. Regs., Part II. and the Staff Manual respectively. Title Pages will be prepared in manuscript.

Place	Date	Hour	Summary of Events and Information	Remarks and references to Appendices
LA CORGUE	22/3/16		Routine Work	
"	23/3/16		" "	
"	24/3/16		" "	
"	25/3/16		" "	
"	26/3/16		" "	
"	27/3/16		Evacuated 20 horses and 1 mule of this division and 1 mule of the 8th Division which were on the march to Authieulle	
"	28/3/16		Routine Work	
"	29/3/16		" "	
"	30/3/16		" "	
"	31/3/16		Evacuated 17 horses and two mules to NEUFCHATEL. Weather during the month has been very changeable and generally unfavourable to horses in the open.	

N Bone Capt. A.V.C.
O.C. 31st Mobile Vet Section

Army Form C. 2118

WAR DIARY
or
INTELLIGENCE SUMMARY 31st Mobile Veterinary Section

(Erase heading not required.)

Place	Date	Hour	Summary of Events and Information	Remarks and references to Appendices
LAGORQUE	1/4/16		Routine Work	
"	2/4/16		" "	
"	3/4/16		" "	
"	4/4/16		Evacuated twenty one horses and two mules to NEUFCHATEL	
"	5/4/16		Routine Work	
"	6/4/16		" "	
"	7/4/16		" "	
"	8/4/16		Evacuated five horses to NEUFCHATEL	
"	9/4/16		Routine Work	
"	10/4/16		Evacuated sixteen horses and four mules to NEUFCHATEL	
"	11/4/16		Routine Work	
"	12/4/16		" "	
"	13/4/16		" "	
"	14/4/16		" "	
"	15/4/16		" "	
"	16/4/16		Evacuated thirty two horses and five mules to NEUFCHATEL. Proceeded to ST HILAIRE to inspect billets in new area.	
"	17/4/16		Section marched to ST VENANT to a billet occupied by the section p. in February	
ST VENANT	18/4/16		Evacuated fourteen horses to NEUFCHATEL	
"	19/4/16		Evacuated forty three horses and two mules to NEUFCHATEL	
"	20/4/16		Routine Work	

Army Form C. 2118

WAR DIARY
or
INTELLIGENCE SUMMARY
(Erase heading not required.)

3/E Mobile Vet. Section. VQ9

XIX   XXX

Place	Date	Hour	Summary of Events and Information	Remarks and references to Appendices
ST VENANT	21/4/15		Section marched to ST HILAIRE about seven miles and 7th was billeted.	
ST HILAIRE	22/4/15		...reached by the Section on the 24/4/15. Routine Work.	
"	23/4/15		"	
"	24/4/15		"	
"	25/4/15		Proceeded with horses and one mule to NEUFCHATEL LILLERS station situated three miles by road from Section. Routine Work.	
"	26/4/15		"	
"	27/4/15		"	
"	28/4/15		Proceeded thirty seven horses and two mules to NEUFCHATEL Routine Work. Collected horse by flint from Rest Camp at about ten miles from Section. Proceeded to THEROUANNE, regarding three horses left there by the 3 9th Division.	
"	29/4/15		Proceeded forty three horses and one mule to NEUFCHATEL	
"	30/4/15		General health of Section during the month good.	

N. Ross Buchanan. A.V.C.
O.C. 31st Mobile Vet Section

Army Form C. 2118

WAR DIARY
or
INTELLIGENCE SUMMARY 3/1st Mobile Vet Section Vol 10
(Erase heading not required.)

Instructions regarding War Diaries and Intelligence Summaries are contained in F.S. Regs., Part II. and the Staff Manual respectively. Title Pages will be prepared in manuscript.

Place	Date	Hour	Summary of Events and Information	Remarks and references to Appendices
ST HILAIRE	1/5/16		Routine Work	
"	2/5/16		Thirty-seven horses and one mule evacuated to NEUFCHATEL	
"	3/5/16		Routine Work	
"	4/5/16		Seventy-eleven horses and two mules to NEUFCHATEL. Collected stray mule from BERGUETTE.	
"	5/5/16		Routine Work	
"	6/5/16		" Arrangements made with O.C. Mobile Vet Section to collect but in area of 19th Division for the collection of horses unserviceable.	
"	7/5/16		Lieut Leland by next autumn.	
"	8/5/16		Routine Work	
"	9/5/16	1.30am	Section marched to AIRE for entrainment to new area. Entrained at 1.35pm. Detrained at LONGUEAU and marched to ST VAST about fifteen kilometres	
LONGUEAU	10/5/16		away about 5 a.m.	
ST VAST	11/5/16		Billeted in a farm and outgoing buildings. Room for horses and men made, new but wants being favourable stabled in Granary. Washing arrangements – arrangement but works for horses hard.	
"	12/5/16		"	
"	13/5/16		"	
"	14/5/16		"	
"	15/5/16		" QED officer check-checked in the division checked and report	
"	16/5/16		forwarded to A.D.V.S.	
"	17/5/16		Routine Work	

Army Form C. 2118

WAR DIARY or INTELLIGENCE SUMMARY

31st Mobile Vet. Section

(Erase heading not required.)

Instructions regarding War Diaries and Intelligence Summaries are contained in F.S. Regs., Part II. and the Staff Manual respectively. Title Pages will be prepared in manuscript.

Place	Date	Hour	Summary of Events and Information	Remarks and references to Appendices
ST VAST	18/5/16		Routine Work. No 542 Sgt Cameron W. AVC joined section temp. reinforced from 89 Bde A.C. on the disbanding of that unit.	
"	19/5/16		Routine Work	
"	20/5/16		Evacuated twenty one horses and three mules from FLESSELLES, ABBEVILLE. Stolen details about one hundred from section.	
"	21/5/16		Routine Work	
"	22/5/16		Routine Work	
"	23/5/16		" "	
"	24/5/16		" "	
"	25/5/16		" "	
"	26/5/16		Evacuated forty five horses and three mules to 1st ABBEVILLE. No 804 Sgt Salu S.C. AVC joined section from 88th Bde A.C. on the disbanding of that unit.	
"	27/5/16		Routine Work	
"	28/5/16		" " Demolished stables at 11.0 pm of Division suspected which had been received by case of mange.	
"	29/5/16		Routine Work	
"	30/5/16		Evacuated eight horses and five mules to ABBEVILLE. During the past month weather has been favourable and general health feeling good.	
"	31/5/16		N. Pine Capt a.V.C. O.C. 31st M.V.S.	

Fuse

Army Form C. 2118

WAR DIARY
or
INTELLIGENCE SUMMARY 3/2nd Mobile Vet. Section Vol II

(Erase heading not required.)

XIX

Instructions regarding War Diaries and Intelligence Summaries are contained in F.S. Regs., Part II. and the Staff Manual respectively. Title Pages will be prepared in manuscript.

Place	Date	Hour	Summary of Events and Information	Remarks and references to Appendices
ST VAST	1/6/16	—	Routine Work	
"	2/6/16	—	" "	
"	3/6/16	—	" "	
"	4/6/16	—	" "	
"	5/6/16	—	Inoculated eight horses to ABBEVILLE	
"	6/6/16	—	Routine Work	
"	7/6/16	—	" "	
"	8/6/16	—	Inoculated six horses & three mules to ABBEVILLE	
"	9/6/16	—	Routine Work	
"	10/6/16	—	" "	
"	11/6/16	—	" "	
"	12/6/16	—	" "	
"	13/6/16	—	" "	
"	14/6/16	—	" "	
"	15/6/16	—	Inoculated fourteen horses and three mules from Lynghés to FORGES-LES-EAUX and six horses three mules from FLESSELLES to ABBEVILLE. Collected on sick horse from a farm at RIVERY near AMIENS.
"	16/6/16	—	Section marched from ST VAST to FRECHENCOURT about eight miles. Billets consist of a few dilapidated buildings and two paddocks, all men under cover, accommodation for about six horses under cover. Working current Rullock about half a mile from billets.
FRECHENCOURT	17/6/16			

WAR DIARY
or
INTELLIGENCE SUMMARY 31st Mobile Vet. Section

Army Form C. 2118

(Erase heading not required.)

Place	Date	Hour	Summary of Events and Information	Remarks and references to Appendices
FRECHENCOURT	18/7/16		Routine Work. Collected a horse from ST VAAST by front.	
"	19/7/16		Sgt. No. 147 Sgt. Geo. 9. transferred to W.V.S.T. HOSPITAL FORGES-LES-EAUX in preparation for Staff Sgt.	
"	20/7/16		Reinvented sundries, horses and mules. Three were referred to return for treatment to No. 7 Vet. Hospital. One NCO and horses evacuating sick horses to Prov. Hospital. Future men-self mobile Vet. Section in the Vicinity of Pte. Ruckhard. On advance all being met.	
"	21/7/16		Convoying sick NCO and full men installed at LAVIEVILLE Relief Works. A party of men sent out to find advance post to Ruckhard by which sick horses will be moved from	
"	22/7/16		With men road traffic. Routine Work	
"	23/7/16		"	
"	24/7/16		Invented more horses and four mules to No. 7 Vet. Hospital.	
"	25/7/16		Routine Work.	
"	26/7/16		"	
"	27/7/16		Invented eight no horses and two mules to No. 7 Vet. Hospital Routine Work	
"	28/7/16		Invented more horses and three mules to No. 7 Vet. Hospital	
"	29/7/16		Section moved from FRECHENCOURT to LAVIEVILLE. All men & equipment attached to Section for evacuating sick horses transferred to No. 16 Mob. Vet. Section. 8th Div.	
	3		Much rain during first month rendering stationing very deep for horses, etc.	

N. Pond Lieut. A.V.C.
O.C. 31st M.V.S.

Army Form C. 2118.

WAR DIARY
or
INTELLIGENCE SUMMARY 31st Mobile Vet. Section

(Erase heading not required.)

Instructions regarding War Diaries and Intelligence Summaries are contained in F.S. Regs., Part II. and the Staff Manual respectively. Title Pages will be prepared in manuscript.

Place	Date	Hour	Summary of Events and Information	Remarks and references to Appendices
LAVIÉVILLE	1/7/16		10 horses and 2 mules evacuated to FORGES-LES-EAUX from MERICOURT. Distance to Railhead about 2½ miles. Conducting parties provided by no 12 Section.	
"	2/7/16		Seven horses and one mule evacuated. Advance foot sanitary section established at ALBERT about three miles from section.	
"	3/7/16		Routine Work.	
"	4/7/16		" "	
"	5/7/16		" "	
"	6/7/16		Evacuated eight horses and few mules. Routine Work	
"	7/7/16		Evacuated eleven horses and his mules. One N.C.O. and one man following attached to the section & set an conducting parties.	
"	8/7/16		Routine Work	
"	9/7/16		" "	
"	10/7/16		Evacuated sixteen horses and five mules. Routine Work	
"	11/7/16		" "	
"	12/7/16			
"	13/7/16		Evacuated nineteen horses and three mules. R.C.O. and one man attached transport	
"	14/7/16		to no 12 M.V.S. MERICOURT. Routine Work.	
"	15/7/16		Evacuated Thirty-Seven horses and two mules.	
"	16/7/16		Routine Work.	
"	17/7/16			

Army Form C. 2118.

WAR DIARY
or
INTELLIGENCE SUMMARY

(Erase heading not required.)

31st Mobile Vet. Section

VO12

Place	Date	Hour	Summary of Events and Information	Remarks and references to Appendices
LAVIÉVILLE	18/7/16		Evacuated thirty horses and two mules. Routine Work.	
"	19/7/16		" "	
"	20/7/16			
"	21/7/16		Evacuated nineteen horses. Section marched to advance ? at ALBERT	
"	22/7/16		Evacuated Public horses and three mules.	
ALBERT	23/7/16		Section returned to LAVIÉVILLE. Advance post established on the RUE DE PERONNE about one mile east of ALBERT. Evacuated twenty-two horses and one mule.	
"	24/7/16			
LAVIÉVILLE	25/7/16		Eighteen horses and three mules evacuated	
"	26/7/16		Fourteen horses and three mules evacuated	
"	27/7/16		Twenty horses and seven mules evacuated	
"	28/7/16		Routine Work	
"	29/7/16		Ten horses and three mules evacuated	
"	30/7/16		Routine Work	
"	31/7/16		Evacuated eleven horses and three mules.	

H. Dow Capt. A.V.C.
O.C. 31st M.V.S.

Army Form C. 2118.

Vol 13

31st Mobile Vet. Section

WAR DIARY
or
INTELLIGENCE SUMMARY
(Erase heading not required.)

Instructions regarding War Diaries and Intelligence Summaries are contained in F. S. Regs., Part II. and the Staff Manual respectively. Title Pages will be prepared in manuscript.

Place	Date	Hour	Summary of Events and Information	Remarks and references to Appendices
LAVIEVILLE	1/8/16		Routine Work	
"	2/8/16		Evacuated 1.23 horses and 1 mule to FORGES-LES-EAUX. No 1567 U.P. acting Sgt. Pollock W. joined the section from 19th D.A.C. Section marched to FREEHENCOURT.	
FRECHENCOURT	3/8/16		Section marched to LONG.	
LONG	4/8/16		Routine Work. No 1567 U.P. acting Sgt. Pollock W. transferred to No 2 Vet. Hospital HAVRE.	
LONG	5/8/16		"	
"	6/8/16		Evacuated three horses by road to ABBEVILLE	
"	7/8/16		Section marched to PONT REMY and entrained for BAILLEUL, arriving at BAILLEUL at 10.30 p.m. Proceeding own to WESTOUTRE	
WESTOUTRE	8/8/16		On billets occupied by the personnel by the 50th Division M.V.S, consisting of eight huts for the men etc. and a stable capable of accommodating thirty-two horses.	
"	9/8/16		Routine work.	
"	10/8/16		"	
"	11/8/16		Evacuated 9 horses to NEUFCHATEL from WIPPENHOEK railhead. Railhead situated about three miles from section. No 2399 Pte Jones L. joined from Pte Smith James for instruction in cold shoeing.	
"	12/8/16		Routine Work.	
"	13/8/16		"	
"	14/8/16		Evacuated 14 horses and 1 mule by road to ST. OMER - distance about twenty-five miles. Rest halt at BORRE and EBLINGHEM. Pte 4532 Pte Wood joined from 57 M.G.C. for instruction in cold shoeing.	
"	15/8/16		Routine Work.	

Army Form C. 2118.

WAR DIARY
or
INTELLIGENCE SUMMARY 31st Mobile Vet. Section

(Erase heading not required.)

Instructions regarding War Diaries and Intelligence Summaries are contained in F. S. Regs., Part II. and the Staff Manual respectively. Title Pages will be prepared in manuscript.

Place	Date	Hour	Summary of Events and Information	Remarks and references to Appendices
WESTOUTRE	16/8/16	—	Routine Work.	
"	17/8/16	—	" No 13325 Cpl. Lawson H.J. attacked for inclusion in cold shoeing	
"	18/8/16	—	"	
"	19/8/16	—	" Dvr. O/2 + 345 Worn F.g. admitted with injuries to 88th Field Amb.	
"	20/8/16	—	Evacuated 18 horses and 7 mules to NEUFCHATEL	
"	21/8/16	—	Routine Work. Dvr J./923 Pullman E. joined from H guards Coy of the Br. Train	
"	22/8/16	—	"	
"	23/8/16	—	"	
"	24/8/16	—	" No 13638 Pte Crockford W.P. joined for inclusion in cold shoeing from 88th M.G.C.	
"	25/8/16	—	Routine Work	
"	26/8/16	—	" No 466 P. Ading Sgt. Wooley admitted to 88th Field Ambulance	
"	27/8/16	—	"	
"	28/8/16	—	"	
"	29/8/16	—	Evacuated 21 horses and 3 mules to HOMER	
"	30/8/16	—	"	
"	31/8/16	—	"	

JB ong Lt
Oc. 31st
M.V.S.

Army Form C. 2118.

WAR DIARY
or
INTELLIGENCE SUMMARY

31st Ed. Mobile Vet Section Vol 14

(Erase heading not required.)

Instructions regarding War Diaries and Intelligence Summaries are contained in F. S. Regs., Part II. and the Staff Manual respectively. Title Pages will be prepared in manuscript.

Place	Date	Hour	Summary of Events and Information	Remarks and references to Appendices
WESTOUTRE	1/9/16		Routine Work	
"	2/9/16		" "	
"	3/9/16		" "	
"	4/9/16		Evacuated 39 horses and 3 mules to St OMER by road	
"	5/9/16		Routine Work	
"	6/9/16		Section moved to new billets at NIEPPE, previous received by O36 F.M.V.S.	
NIEPPE	7/9/16		Routine Work. New billets incomplete 40 horse mule van and ready-up open lined standing, all work field on R.E. hds. a good water supply for horse and men	
NIEPPE	8/9/16		Routine Work	
"	9/9/16		" "	
"	10/9/16		Routine Work	
"	11/9/16		" " Sgt Briggs No 4094 9 Vet joined	
"	12/9/16		" " Capt Hollis ? cattle extolled	
"	13/9/16		Evacuated 8 horses by Barge from BAC ST MAUR to ST OMER	
"	14/9/16		Evacuated 45 horses by road to ST OMER	
"	15/9/16		Routine Work	
"	16/9/16		Evacuated 14 horses and 1 mule from ESTAIRES by Barge to ST OMER	
"	17/9/16		Routine Work	
"	18/9/16		Evacuated 6 horses at 2 miles from BAC ST MAUR to ST OMER and 6 21 horses 9 mules by road to ST OMER	
"	19/9/16		Routine Work	
"	20/9/16		Evacuated 9 horses and 4 mules from BAC ST MAUR to ST OMER	
"	21/9/16			

Army Form C. 2118.

WAR DIARY
or
INTELLIGENCE SUMMARY

(Erase heading not required.)

31st Mobile Vet Section

Instructions regarding War Diaries and Intelligence Summaries are contained in F. S. Regs., Part II. and the Staff Manual respectively. Title Pages will be prepared in manuscript.

Place	Date	Hour	Summary of Events and Information	Remarks and references to Appendices
NIEPPE	22/9/16		Routine Work	
"	23/9/16		" "	
"	24/9/16		Evacuated 10 horses from ESTAIRES	
"	25/9/16		Routine Work	
"	26/9/16		11 horses evacuated from BAC ST MAUR	
"	27/9/16		Routine Work	
"	28/9/16		11 horses and 2 mules evacuated from BAC ST MAUR. A.V.T 4/1442.33 & 72/1806 2/Lt Hawkins O.C. A.S.C	
"	29/9/16		Routine Work & T 4/1442.33 2/Lt Prestgard Off: O. A.S.C.	
"	30/9/16		" "	

N. Powe Capt. A.V.C.
O.C. 31st M.V.S.
O.C. 31st M.V. Div.
19

Army Form C. 2118.

WAR DIARY
or
INTELLIGENCE SUMMARY

3/ MOBILE VETERINARY SECTION
Vol 14

(Erase heading not required.)

Place	Date	Hour	Summary of Events and Information	Remarks and references to Appendices
NIEPPE	1.10.16		Evacuated 17 horses & 4 mules by train from ESTAIRES to ST OMER	
	2.10.16		" 40 " — — — by road to ST OMER	
VIEUX-BERQUIN	3.10.16		Section marched from NIEPPE to VIEUX-BERQUIN	
	4.10.16		Routine work.	
	5.10.16		ditto	
	6.10.16		Section moved from VIEUX-BERQUIN to BAILLEUL WEST & entrained to DOULLENS.	
AUTHIE	7.10.16		Detrained & marched to AUTHIE.	
	8.10.16		Routine work.	
	9.10.16		ditto	
	10.10.16		ditto	
	11.10.16		ditto	
	12.10.16		Evacuated 23 horses & 2 mules to ABBEVILLE from BELLE EGLISE Radis 150R; No 11445 PTE SMITH W. A.V.C. transferred to No 23 VETY. HOSPITAL, ST.OMER.	
	13.10.16		Evacuated 56 horses to ABBEVILLE	
	14.10.16		Routine work	
	15.10.16		Evacuated 40 horses & 1 mule to ABBEVILLE	
	16.10.16		Routine work.	
	17.10.16		Section marched from AUTHIE to CONTAY	
CONTAY	18.10.16		Evacuated 10 horses & 6 mules to ABBEVILLE	
	19.10.16		Routine work.	
	20.10.16		ditto	
	21.10.16		Section moved from CONTAY to BOUZINCOURT	

Army Form C. 2118.

WAR DIARY
or
INTELLIGENCE SUMMARY
(Erase heading not required.)

Instructions regarding War Diaries and Intelligence Summaries are contained in F. S. Regs., Part II. and the Staff Manual respectively. Title Pages will be prepared in manuscript.

Place	Date	Hour	Summary of Events and Information	Remarks and references to Appendices
BOULINCOURT	22.10.16		Routine work	
	23.10.16		ditto ; 1 N.C.O & 4 MEN joined the section from 37th M.V.S. as conducting parties.	
	24.10.16		Evacuated 30 horses & 7 mules from ALBERT to FORGES-LES-EAUX.	
	25.10.16		" 16 " 13 " " " "	
	26.10.16		" 21 " 1 " " " "	
	27.10.16		No 7973 PTE BROWN H. A.V.C. joined section from NO 13 VETY HOSPITAL to complete establishment	
			Routine work	
	28.10.16		Evacuated 30 horses & 2 mules from ALBERT to FORGES-LES-EAUX.	
	29.10.16		" 19 " 3 " " " "	
	30.10.16		" 21 " 3 " " " "	
			NO 365 SERGT GURMAN R.W A.V.C. reduced to the ranks.	
			CAPT. H. BONE- left section to join 8th DIVISION.	
			CAPT. A.R. SMYTH E. A.V.C. took over command of the section.	
			Routine work.	
	31.10.16		No 71/336 Dvr SMITH W. A.S.C. despatched to A.S.C. BASE DEPOT, HAVRE for transfer to home establishment	

A.R. Smythe Capt. A.V.C.
O.C.
31st M.V.S.

Army Form C. 2118.

WAR DIARY
or
INTELLIGENCE SUMMARY

3/2 M.V.S.

Vol 16

(Erase heading not required.)

Place	Date	Hour	Summary of Events and Information	Remarks and references to Appendices
BOUZINCOURT	1.11.16		Evacuated 59 horses & 5 mules to FORGES-LES-EAUX.	
	2.11.16		Pte. CROCKFORD. W. D. 5/8¹⁴ M.G.Coy & Pte JONES. 7¹ˢᵗ S. LANCS.R transf'd. SCHOOL of FARRIERY. ABBEVILLE	
	3.11.16		Evacuated 50 horses & 6 mules.	
	4.11.16		Routine work.	
	5.11.16		Evacuated 54 horses 18 mules.	
	6.11.16		Routine work.	
	7.11.16		Evacuated 36 horses & 6 mules.	
	8.11.16		" 26 " 6 "	
	9.11.16		" 33 " 7 "	
	10.11.16		" 24 " 8 "	
	11.11.16		" 40 " 2 "	
	12.11.16		No 5766 Sergeant HOWE.S. joined from No 10 VET. HOSPITAL to complete establishment	
	12.11.16		Evacuated 36 horses 14 mules.	
	13.11.16		" " 36 " 4 "	
	14.11.16		" " 29 " 3 "	
	15.11.16		" " 41 " 7 "	
	16.11.16		" " 31 " 1 "	
	17.11.16		Sgt. GURMAN. R.W. No 365 transf'd No 1 Vety. HOSPITAL. Routine work.	

Army Form C. 2118.

WAR DIARY
or
INTELLIGENCE SUMMARY

2.

(Erase heading not required.)

Instructions regarding War Diaries and Intelligence Summaries are contained in F.S. Regs., Part II. and the Staff Manual respectively. Title Pages will be prepared in manuscript.

Place	Date	Hour	Summary of Events and Information	Remarks and references to Appendices
BOUZINCOURT	16.11.16		Evacuated 23 horses & 9 mules to FORGES-LES-EAUX. No 863, Pte LAMBOURNE.G transfd to 12th LANCERS.	
	19.11.16		Evacuated 19 horses & 5 mules.	
	20.11.16		Routine work.	
	21.11.16		Evacuated 9 horses & 4 mules.	
	22.11.16		3 ,, 12 ,, ,,	
	23.11.16		Section marched to CONTAY.	
	24.11.16		,, ,, ,, from ,, to DOULLENS.	
			,, ,, ,, DOULLENS to BERNAVILLE.	
BERNAVILLE	25.11.16		Routine work.	
	26.11.16		,, ,,	
	27.11.16		,, ,,	
	28.11.16		,, ,,	
	29.11.16		,, ,,	
	30.11.16		,, ,,	

Army Form C. 2118.

WAR DIARY
or
INTELLIGENCE SUMMARY

31. M. V. S. (1)

Vol 17

(Erase heading not required.)

Instructions regarding War Diaries and Intelligence Summaries are contained in F. S. Regs., Part II. and the Staff Manual respectively. Title Pages will be prepared in manuscript.

Place	Date	Hour	Summary of Events and Information	Remarks and references to Appendices
BERNAVILLE	1-12-16		Routine work	
	2-12-16		" "	
	3-12-16		" "	
	4-12-16		" "	
	5-12-16		" "	
	6-12-16		" "	
	7-12-16		Evacuated 17 horses & 6 mules to Abbeville	
	8-12-16		Routine work. No. 9357 Pte. Early, R. joined from no. 12 Vet. Hosp. to complete establishment	
	9-12-16		Routine work	
	10-12-16		" "	
	11-12-16		" "	
	12-12-16		" "	
	13-12-16		" "	
	14-12-16		Evacuated 30 horses & 3 mules to Abbeville	
	15-12-16		Routine work. No. 4301 Pte. Aurach, E. joined for instruction in cold shoeing from 56th M.G. Coy. No. 19358 Pte. Relly and A.H. joined from 10th	
	16-12-16		" "	
	17-12-16		Worked on for instruction in cold shoeing	
	18-12-16		Routine work	
	19-12-16		" "	
	20-12-16		" "	
	21-12-16		Evacuated 20 horses & 1 mule to Abbeville	
	22-12-16		Routine work	

Army Form C. 2118.

WAR DIARY
or
INTELLIGENCE SUMMARY

(Erase heading not required.)

(2)

Instructions regarding War Diaries and Intelligence Summaries are contained in F. S. Regs., Part II. and the Staff Manual respectively. Title Pages will be prepared in manuscript.

Place	Date	Hour	Summary of Events and Information	Remarks and references to Appendices
BERNAVILLE	23-12-16		Routine work No 7975 Pte. Brown. H. evacuated sick	
	24-12-16		" "	
	25-12-16		" "	
	26-12-16		" "	
	27-12-16		" "	
	28-12-16		" " Capt. A.R. Smyth granted leave to 6-1-17	
	29-12-16		" " S.S. Kerr took over duties as O.C. 31st M.V.S.	
			No. 11837 Pte. Jones A.J. M.O. N.I.S.D. joined for instruction in cold shoeing	
			from Q.P.M. M. ?(H.D.D.)? Routine work.	
	30-12-16		Evacuated 25 horses & 3 mules to Abbeville. No 4301 Pte Awarke	
	31-12-16		No. 19358 Pte. Bergand. H. No. 11837 Pte. Jones. A.J. transferred	
			to school of Farriery Abbeville for further instruction.	

S.S. Kerr. Capt. A.V.C.

Army Form C. 2118

WAR DIARY
or
INTELLIGENCE SUMMARY
(Erase heading not required.)

1. 31 M Vety Sec
Vol 18

Place	Date	Hour	Summary of Events and Information	Remarks and references to Appendices
BERNAVILLE	1.1.17		} Routine work.	
	2.1.17			
	3.1.17			
	4.1.17			
	5.1.17			
	6.1.17		Evacuated 36 horses & 1 mule to Abbeville	
	7.1.17		} Routine work.	
	8.1.17			
	9.1.17		Section marched from Bernaville to Authie	
AUTHIE	10.1.17		Routine work	
	11.1.17		ditto	
	12.1.17		Evacuated 44 horses & 3 Mules to Abbeville. 70704 Flynn J. Pte. joined from No 2 Veterinary Hospital	
	13.1.17		} Routine work	
	14.1.17			
	15.1.17			
	16.1.17		Evacuated 45 horses & 6 Mules.	
	17.1.17		} Routine work.	
	18.1.17			
	19.1.17			

Army Form C. 2118

WAR DIARY
or
INTELLIGENCE SUMMARY
(Erase heading not required.)

2.

Instructions regarding War Diaries and Intelligence Summaries are contained in F.S. Regs., Part II. and the Staff Manual respectively. Title Pages will be prepared in manuscript.

Place	Date	Hour	Summary of Events and Information	Remarks and references to Appendices
	20.1.17		Evacuated 25 horses to Abbeville.	
	21.1.17		Routine work	
	22.1.17			
	23.1.17			
	24.1.17		Evacuated 26 horses to Abbeville	
	25.1.17		Routine work	
	26.1.17			
	27.1.17		ditto	
			No 36790 Pte. Britland J. 7th Bn East Lancs. Regt. posted for instruction in Cold Shoeing.	
	28.1.17		Routine work	
	29.1.17		ditto	
			No. 13640 Dvr. Wilson V. 7th Bn. K.O.R.L. Regt. posted for instruction in Cold Shoeing	
	30.1.17		Routine work.	
	31.1.17		31 Horses Evacuated to Abbeville	
			No 36790 Pte. Britland J. and No 13640 Dvr. Wilson V transferred to School of Farriery Abbeville	

J.R.Smythe Capt. A.V.C.
O.C. 31st M.V.S.

Army Form C. 2118

WAR DIARY
or
INTELLIGENCE SUMMARY

(Erase heading not required.)

3/- M.V.S. Vol 19

Place	Date	Hour	Summary of Events and Information	Remarks and references to Appendices
AUTHIE	1.2.17		Routine work	
	2.2.17			
	3.2.17			
	4.2.17			
	5.2.17			
	6.2.17			
	7.2.17			
	8.2.17			
	9.2.17			
	10.2.17			
	11.2.17			
	12.2.17		Evacuated 24 horses from Belle Eglise to Abbeville.	
	13.2.17		Routine work.	
	14.2.17		Evacuated 35 horses & 3 mules from Belle Eglise to Abbeville. No 17634 Sgt. Harrison C.A.V.C. joined from B.B./ty 88th Bde R.F.A.	
	15.2.17		Routine work.	
	16.2.17		Evacuated 38 horses from Belle Eglise to Abbeville. No 17634 Sgt. Harrison C.A.V.C. transferred to No 3 Veterinary Hospital	
	17.2.17		Routine work	
	18.2.17			

Army Form C. 2118

WAR DIARY
or
INTELLIGENCE SUMMARY

(Erase heading not required.)

Instructions regarding War Diaries and Intelligence Summaries are contained in F.S. Regs., Part II. and the Staff Manual respectively. Title Pages will be prepared in manuscript.

Place	Date	Hour	Summary of Events and Information	Remarks and references to Appendices
RUTHIE	19.2.17		Evacuated 9 horses & 1 mule to Abbeville from Belle Eglise.	
	20.2.17		Routine work	
	21.2.17		Section moved from Ruthie to Bus-les-Artois.	
Bus-les- Artois	22.2.17		Routine work.	
	23.2.17		Evacuated 20 horses + 3 mules from Belle Eglise.	
	24.2.17		} Routine work.	
	25.2.17			
	26.2.17		Routine work No 13299 Pte. Fiddler. E. 7th L.N.Lancs Regt. No 12586 Pte Wills T. 7th L. Lancs Rgt. joined section for instruction in cold shoeing.	
	27.2.17		Routine work. No 17712 Pte Freeman W. 5th Bn. L.W.B. joined section for course of instruction in cold shoeing.	
	28.2.17		Evacuated 24 horses + 8 mules to Abbeville from Beauval. No 12586 Pte Wills T. + 17712 Pte Freeman W. proceeded to School of Farriery at Abbeville.	

A.R. Smythe Capt. A.V.C.
O.C. 31 ♢M.V.S.

Army Form C. 2118.

WAR DIARY
or
INTELLIGENCE SUMMARY 31 M.V.S Vol 20

L.

(Erase heading not required.)

Instructions regarding War Diaries and Intelligence Summaries are contained in F. S. Regs., Part II. and the Staff Manual respectively. Title Pages will be prepared in manuscript.

Place	Date	Hour	Summary of Events and Information	Remarks and references to Appendices
Bus-les-ARTOIS	1/3/17		Routine work.	
	2/3/17		Evacuated 14 horses & two mules from Beauval Station to No 22 Vety. Hospital Abbeville	
	3/3/17		Routine work	
	4/3/17			
	5/3/17			
	6/3/17			
	7/3/17		Evacuated 23 horses from Beauval & Abbeville	
	8/3/17		Routine work	
	9/3/17		Evacuated 21 horses & 6 mules from Beauval to Abbeville	
	10/3/17		Transferred 11 horses & 3 mules to 12th M.V.S. for evacuation.
			" 10 " " 2 " " 41st " " "
Sercus moved	11/3/17		Section marched from Bus to Sercus.	
	12/3/17		" " " Sercus & moved.	
Mazinghem	13/3/17		" " " moved to Mazinghem.	
	14/3/17		Routine work.	

Army Form C. 2118.

WAR DIARY
or
INTELLIGENCE SUMMARY

(Erase heading not required.)

II.

Instructions regarding War Diaries and Intelligence Summaries are contained in F. S. Regs., Part II. and the Staff Manual respectively. Title Pages will be prepared in manuscript.

Place	Date	Hour	Summary of Events and Information	Remarks and references to Appendices
St Hilaire Cottes	15/3/17		Section marched from Haynecourt to St Hilaire Cottes.	
	16/3/17		Routine work	
Steenbecque	17/3/17		Marched from St Hilaire to Steenbecque.	
Nieurlet	18/3/17		Marched from Steenbecque to Nieurlet.	
Leuf Bergnin	19/3/17		Marched from Nieurlet to Leuf Bergnin.	
Isebre	20/3/17		Marched from Leuf Bergnin to Isebre.	
	21/3/17			
	22/3/17			
	23/3/17		Routine work.	
	24/3/17			
	25/3/17		Evacuated 2 Horses & 2 Mules to No 23 Veterinary Hospital St Omer	
	26.3.17		Routine work	
	27/3/17			
	28/3/17		Evacuated 4 Horses & 3 Mules to Mules by road to St Omer.	
	29/3/17		Routine work. 2 " Motor Ambulance	
Lealinthe	30/3/17		Section marched from Isebre to Lealinthe.	
	31/3/17			

WAR DIARY or INTELLIGENCE SUMMARY

Army Form C. 2118.

Sheet I.

Place	Date	Hour	Summary of Events and Information	Remarks and references to Appendices
Westoutre	1917 April 1		Moved to No. 15. C. C. S. at 6. Sheet 28. R. Rankine Won R. to 6359 Pte. Hume.	
	2.		Rejoined from hospital.	
	3.		Routine work. 6491 Cpl. Hilton. C.E. placed under arrest	
	4.		Routine work. 6491 Cpl. Hilton. C.E. admitted to 59 F.L. Ambulance.	
	5.		Routine work.	
	6.		Routine work.	
	7.		Routine work.	
	8.		Routine work.	
	9.		Routine work.	
	10.		Routine work.	
	11.		3 horses 3 mules sent by road to No 23rd. Veterinary Hospital. 2 horses 10 mules per motor ambulance to No 28 Veterinary Hospital, St. Omer.	
	12.		Routine work.	
	13.		Routine work.	
	14.		Routine work. 2/3291 Pte. Whelan (A.V.C.) admitted to 59 F. Field Ambulance.	
	15.		Routine work.	
	16.		Routine work.	
	17.		Routine work.	
	18.		Routine work. 15 horses 13 mules to 23rd. Veterinary Hospital, St. Omer.	
	19.		Routine work. No. 6491 Cpl. Hilton. C.E. returned to duty. 1907 Pte. Brown. C. proceeded on ten days special leave.	

Army Form C. 2118.

WAR DIARY
or
INTELLIGENCE SUMMARY
(Erase heading not required.)

Place	Date	Hour	Summary of Events and Information	Remarks and references to Appendices
Westoutre	April 1.		Moved to 13. C.M.D. Sheet 28. Routine work to 6339 Pte. Hume R. rejoined from hospital.	
	2.		Routine work. 6491 Cpl. Hinton C.E. placed under arrest. (59 K.)	
	3.		" " " admitted to Liera arrt.	
	4.		" " "	
	5.		" " "	
	6.		" " "	
	7.		" " "	
	8.		" " "	
	9.		" " "	
	10.		" " "	
	11.		3) horses & 3 mules by road to 23 Veterinary Hospital 2 " & 10 " " motor ambulance to 23 Vety. Hospital Routine work.	
	12.		" " "	
	13.		" " "	
	14.		2/3201 Pr. W. Tetan. W. (A.S.C.) to 59 K. Field ambulance	
	15.		" " "	
	16.		" " "	
	17.		" horses & 3 mules to 23 Veterinary Hospital	
	18.		6491 Cpl. Hinton. C.E. returned to duty. 1907 Pte.	
	19.		Brown. C. proceeded on Coorat team to 5 days.	

Army Form C. 2118.

WAR DIARY
or
INTELLIGENCE SUMMARY

(Erase heading not required.)

Sheet 2

Instructions regarding War Diaries and Intelligence Summaries are contained in F. S. Regs., Part II. and the Staff Manual respectively. Title Pages will be prepared in manuscript.

Place	Date	Hour	Summary of Events and Information	Remarks and references to Appendices
Seadowell	April 1917 19.		Routine work. To O.H.Q. Cpl. Hixon C. admitted to Sgt. Field Ambulance.	
	20.			
	21.		Routine work. 464 Pte. Heath A. & O+g Pte. Shippard A. admitted to Sgt. Field Ambulance. Cpl. +3 men temporarily attached to II Corps Mobile Veterinary detachment.	
	22.		Routine work R.	
	23.		Routine work R.	
	24.		Routine work R.	
	25.		Routine work R. 6 Mules to 1023 Veterinary Hospital, St. Omer.	
	26.		Routine work R. 24 horses 44 mules to 1025 Veterinary Hospital.	
	27.		Routine work R.	
	28.		Routine work R.	
	29.		Routine work R.	
	30.		Routine work R.	

A. Smythe.
Capt. A.V.C.
O.C. 3rd M.V.S.

Army Form C. 2118.

Sheet II.

WAR DIARY
or
INTELLIGENCE SUMMARY
(Erase heading not required.)

Instructions regarding War Diaries and Intelligence Summaries are contained in F. S. Regs., Part II. and the Staff Manual respectively. Title Pages will be prepared in manuscript.

Place	Date 1917 April	Hour	Summary of Events and Information	Remarks and references to Appendices
Westoutre	20.		Routine work. 6 + 9. Cpl. Kirton. C. E. admitted to 59 F. Ambulance sick.	
"	21.		Pte. theat. A.J. & 6 of 59 Pte. Whipped. A. admitted to 59 F. Field Ambulance. Cpl. 83 Private's temporarily attached to 5th Corps motor Ammunition detachment.	
"	22.		"	
"	23.		"	
"	24.		6 Riders to 23 Veterinary Hospital, St. Omer.	
"	25.		24 Horses & 4 mules to 23rd Veterinary Hospital. 21/SR/928 Pr. Robinson. E. (A.V.C.) reported for duty from 13th Co. A.V.C.	
"	26.		"	
"	27.		"	
"	28.		"	
"	29.		"	
"	30.		"	

A.S. Sugh[?] Capt. A.V.C.
O.C. 31st Mo.V.S.
14/7/17.

Army Form C. 2118.

WAR DIARY
or
INTELLIGENCE SUMMARY

(Erase heading not required.)

Mot Vely See

Place	Date 1917	Hour	Summary of Events and Information	Remarks and references to Appendices
Westoutre.	Sept. 1	.	Routine work. 3540 S.S. Beck. J. admitted to 59th. Field Ambulance. 287 Pte. Heast. Q. returned to duty from 59th. Field Ambulance. Corporal & 3 men returned from IX Corps Mobile Veterinary Detachment.	
Poperinghe	2.	.	2/Lt. C.D.J. Steet 28. 190 Pte. Brown. C. returned from special leave. 13 horses landed over by 35 Mobile Veterinary Section on relief.	
	3.	.	Routine work.	
	4.	.	Routine work. 1410 Pte. Roxford. S. awarded 14 days C.B. & forfeit 10 days pay. 6439 Pte. Liefield. Q. returned to duty from 59th. Field Ambulance.	
	5.	.	Routine work. 639 Pte. Owens. H. admitted to 59th. St. Ambulance. 2 horses & 2 riders to 23rd. Veterinary Hospital, St. Omer.	
	6.	.	Routine work.	
	7.	.	Routine work. 3540 S.S. Beck. J. transferred to 53rd. C.C.S.	
	8.	.	Routine work. 6491 Cpl. Hinton. C.E. transferred to Base sick.	
	9.	.	Routine work.	
	10.	.	Routine work.	
Westoutre.	11.	.	Moves to M.16.a. S.S. Sheet 28.	
	12.	.	Routine work.	
	13.	.	Routine work. 11839 Pte. (A/L/Cpl.) Robson. P. for duty from 203 Veterinary Hospital, Boulogne.	
	14.	.	Routine work.	
	15.	.	Routine work. Fr. Lee admitted to 59th. Field Ambulance. 71054 Sr. Patrickson. W. for duty from to 3 Section. 19th. D.A.C. 20900 P/A/ Cpl. Brown. G. transferred to 109th. Luftsde. 36th. Division.	
	16.	1	Routine work. 5802 Dr. Lee. G. discharged from 59th. Field Ambulance.	

Army Form C. 2118.

WAR DIARY
or
INTELLIGENCE SUMMARY

(Erase heading not required.)

Instructions regarding War Diaries and Intelligence Summaries are contained in F. S. Regs., Part II. and the Staff Manual respectively. Title Pages will be prepared in manuscript.

Place	Date 1917 May	Hour	Summary of Events and Information	Remarks and references to Appendices
Wadoube	17.	.	Routine work. By D.O.C. 19 Division. Pte. Heath. A. admitted to 59th F. Ambulance. Inspection	
	18.	.	Routine work. Acting A.D.V.S. while A.D.V.S. on leave.	
	19.	.	Routine work.	
	20.	.	Routine work.	
	21.	.	Routine work. Corporal & 3 men temporarily transferred to 18 Corps Mobile Veterinary Section.	
	22.	.	Routine work.	
	23.	.	Routine work. 10 horses & 7 mules to 23rd. Veterinary Hospital, St. Omer. 61478 Pte. Cagle. E. for duty from 10 4 Veterinary Hospital, Calais.	
	24.	.	Routine work. 639 Pte. Stevens. H. transferred to 12 C.C.S.	
	25.	.	Routine work.	
	26.	.	Routine work. To S.P. 10 S.S. Queen E. for duty from 10 6 Veterinary Hospital, Rouen.	
	27.	.	Routine work. 10787 Pte. Heart. A. discharged from 59th Field Ambulance.	
	28.	.	Routine work. 5 horse hides to 23rd. Veterinary Hospital, St. Omer.	
	29.	.	Routine work.	
	30.	.	Routine work. 33 horses & 2 mules to 23rd. Veterinary Hospital, St. Omer.	
	31.	.	Routine work.	

N.P. Smythe
Capt. A.V.C.
O.C. 31st. Aux V.S.
1.6.17.

Army Form C. 2118.

WAR DIARY
or
INTELLIGENCE SUMMARY

(Erase heading not required.)

31 Mob Vety Hosp

Vol 23

Place	Date	Hour	Summary of Events and Information	Remarks and references to Appendices
Westoutre	1-6-17		Routine work	
"	2-6-17		"	
"	3-6-17		No SR 10 Shoeing Smith Ansell. F. admitted to 59 F. Amb.	
"	4-6-17		" 2 Horses & 7 Mules to 23 Vet. Hosp.	
"	5-6-17		" & 7 Mules to 23 " "	
"	6-6-17		" 35 " " " " No. T4/144233 Dr Bridgwater. O.	
"	7-6-17		Granted leave.	
"	8-6-17			
"	9-6-17		24 Horses & 6 Mules to 9th Corps M.V.D. No 6339 Pte. Hume R	
"	10-6-17		Granted leave. Corporal & 1 Men temporarily detached to 9th Corps M.V.D.	
"	11-6-17			
"	12-6-17		1 Horse 1 Mule & 8 Mules to 23rd Vet Hosp. No 24 380 Pte. Gordon A.G. for duty from No. 1 Vet Hosp.	
"	13-6-17		18 Horses & Mules to 23rd Vet. Hosp.	
"	14-6-17		Moved to Locre. Map ref. M23.C.6.d. No.639 Pte Nevens H. to No 1 Vet. Hosp.	
Locre	15-6-17		Routine work 1 Horse & 2 Mules to 9th Corps M.V.D.	
"	16-6-17		"	
"	17-6-17		"	
"	18-6-17		Moved to St Jans Capelle. Map ref. S/d.1.4.	
"	19-6-17		Routine work. No 3201 Shoeing Smith Henderson. J. from 23rd Vet. Hosp.	
Sjans Capelle	20-6-17		" " No.T4/144233 Dr Bridgwater. O. returned from leave.	
"	21-6-17			

Army Form C. 2118.

WAR DIARY
or
INTELLIGENCE SUMMARY

(Erase heading not required.)

Instructions regarding War Diaries and Intelligence Summaries are contained in F. S. Regs., Part II. and the Staff Manual respectively. Title Pages will be prepared in manuscript.

Place	Date	Hour	Summary of Events and Information	Remarks and references to Appendices
Hans Capelle	22-6-17		Routine work no 6339 Pt Hume R. returned from leave.	
"	23-6-17		"	
"	24-6-17		"	
"	25-6-17		"	
"	26-6-17		"	
"	27-6-17		"	
"	28-6-17		16 horses & 5 mules to 9th Corps M.V.D.	
"	29-6-17		1 mule & 0 hides to 9th Corps M.V.D. Capt Q.R. Smythe granted leave. Capt. D.S. Kerr A.V.C. took over 31st M.V.S.	
"	30-6-17		"	

D.S. Kerr, Capt. A.V.C.
for O.C., 31st M.V.S.

WAR DIARY
or
INTELLIGENCE SUMMARY

(Erase heading not required.)

Army Form C. 2118.

Place	Date 1919	Hour	Summary of Events and Information	Remarks and references to Appendices
At far Capel.	July 1.	—	Routine work.	
Lapre	2.	"	" "	
	3.	"	Moved to hr. 23. c. 5. 2.	
	4.	"	Routine work. 9354 Pte. Lawley. P. to 48th Field Ambulance	
	5.	"	" 6339 " Hume. R. " 5'7 Ry.	
	6.	"	" 9354 " Lawley. R. transferred to 53rd. C.C.S.	
	7.	"	"	
	8.	"	"	
	9.	"	" Capt. O/P. Smythe. (A.V.C.) returned from leave.	
	10.	"	"	
	11.	"	"	
	12.	"	"	
	13.	"	"	
	14.	"	"	
	15.	"	" 31 horses & 10 mules to 23 Veterinary Hospital. 7074 Pte. Lynn. J. to 67 Ry. Field Ambulance. 393 P/A/C/Sgt. Jubb. H.T. for duty from 34 K. Inf. T.3.	
	16.	"	" 6339 Pte. Hume. R. returned to duty.	
	17.	"	" 7074 Pte. Lynn. J. returned to duty.	

Army Form C. 2118.

WAR DIARY
or
INTELLIGENCE SUMMARY

(Erase heading not required.)

Sheet 11

Place	Date 1919 July	Hour	Summary of Events and Information	Remarks and references to Appendices
Laere.	18.		Routine work.	
	19.		"	
	20.		"	
	21.		"	
	22.		" 13 horses & 4 mules to 23 Veterinary Hospital. 5220 Pte. Allen W. proceeded on leave.	
	23.		" 17498 Sr. Harding started from C.J.S. A.S. 3 horses wounded by bomb splinters. 13540 Pte. Roberts J. 9.H.W.C.S.Y. killed by bomb. 16380 Pte. Quirk J. 9.H.R.W. Sus. wounded by bomb.	
	24.		" 1/AR/923 Sr. Robinson E. (A.S.C.) wounded in bomb. 17685 Pte. Bromage W. 9.H.Q.W. Wilts attacked. 16380 Pte. Quirk J. 9.H.Q.W. Sus. died from wounds. 2 horses to 23 Veterinary Hospital	
	25.		"	
	26.		"	
	27.		"	
	28.		"	
	29.		" 13 horses & 5 mules to 23 Veterinary Hospital. 9807 Pte. Lawley R. for duty.	
	30.		"	
	31.		"	

A.J.Smythe Capt. A.V.C.
O.C. S.M.V.S.
1.8.17.

Army Form C. 2118.

WAR DIARY
or
INTELLIGENCE SUMMARY.

(Erase heading not required.)

Mob. Vety. Secn.

Sheet 1.

WD 25

Instructions regarding War Diaries and Intelligence Summaries are contained in F. S. Regs., Part II. and the Staff Manual respectively. Title pages will be prepared in manuscript.

Place	Date 1917	Hour	Summary of Events and Information	Remarks and references to Appendices
Louvre.	August 1st.		Routine work. 23470 Pte. Mitchell. B.8 25+81 Pte. Whitehead Q.A. for duty from 1st Veterinary hospital.	
	2.		" 6539 Pte. Shine. B.8 24300 Pte. Logan Q.A. temporarily to IX corps mobile Vety. detachment.	
	3.		"	
	4.		"	
	5.		" 9 horses 83 mules to 23rd. Veterinary Hospital.	
	6.		"	
	7.		" 6 horses & 2 mules landed over to 37th. M.V.S.	
	8.		" 13 horses to IV corps mobile Vety. detachment.	
St Jean Capel.	9.		moved to.	
Watton Capel.	10.		"	
Argues	11.		"	
Pierces	12.		Routine work.	
Blequin	13.		" 1889 Pte. Thomas S/P.W.B attached for rations.	
	14.		"	
	15.		" 1774 Pte. Brown. L. proceeded on ten days leave period 16/8/17 to 26/8/17.	

Army Form C. 2118.

WAR DIARY
or
INTELLIGENCE SUMMARY.   Sheet II.
(Erase heading not required.)

Place	Date 191	Hour	Summary of Events and Information	Remarks and references to Appendices
Mesples les Bruin	August 16.		Routine work. 24300 Pte. London A.D. transferred to No 2 Veterinary hospital.	
	17.		"	
	18.		" 18381 Pte. Thomas 5/P.W.B. returned to duty	
	19.		"	
	20.		"	
	21.		" 12 horses to 28 vy. Veterinary hospital.	
	22.		"	
	23.		"	
	24.		"	
	25.		"	
	26.		" 5 horses to 28 vy. Veterinary Hospital.	
Argues	27.		moved to.	
Clarke	28.		"	
St. Jans	29.		"	
Capel	30.		Routine work.	
	31.		" 6539 Pte. Thorne P. 25481 Pte. Metcalfe P. 8 65474 Pte. Perry J.R. temporarily to I Corps No. S.S.	

D.A. Smythe Capt. A.V.C.
O.C. 3 Sy. No. V. S.
3/9/17

WAR DIARY
or
INTELLIGENCE SUMMARY.
(Erase heading not required.)

Army Form C. 2118.

31 Ind Vet*y* [?] Sheet 1

Place	Date 1917 Septr.	Hour	Summary of Events and Information	Remarks and references to Appendices
St. Jans Capel	1.		Routine work.	
	2.		"	
	3.		4/108/923 Dr. Robinson, E. (A.V.C.) posting to 9.F. Bttn. Royal Munster Lancs. Regt.	
	4.		"	
	5.		"	
	6.		4/62435 Dr. Bourne, E.S. (A.V.C.) for duty from 15th Coy. A.V.C.	
	7.		3 horses to 23rd. Veterinary Hospital.	
	8.		5 Mules to 23rd. Veterinary Hospital.	
	9.		"	
Locre.	10.		Moved to — (M. 23. C. 5. 2.)	
	11.		Routine work.	
	12.		" 27 horses & 1 mule to 28rd. Vety. Hospital.	
	13.		"	
	14.		"	
	15.		" 1573 Pte. Mitchell, T. proceeded on 10 days leave. 17.9.17 to 27.9.17	
	16.		" 1 horse to IX Corps H.I.	
	17.		" 6541 Pte. Tucker, H. proceeded on 10 days leave. 19.9.17 to 29.9.17	
	18.			

Army Form C. 2118.

WAR DIARY
or
INTELLIGENCE SUMMARY.
(Erase heading not required.)

Sheet 2.

Place	Date 1917 Sept.	Hour	Summary of Events and Information	Remarks and references to Appendices
Laire.	19.		Routine work. 38 horses & 5 mules to 03rd. Vety. Hospital.	
	20.		Routine work. 2 " 8 / " " IX Corps M.T.S.	
	21.		" / horse to VI Corps M.T.S.	
	22.		" "	
	23.		" "	
	24.		" "	
	25.		" 24 horses 3 mules to 23rd. Vety. Hospital	
	26.		" 1 horses to IX Corps M.T.S.	
	27.		" 1 horse 8 /	
	28.		" 1673 Pte. Shirlock L. returned from leave.	
	29.		" 2 horses to IX Corps M.T.S.	
	30.		" 6541 Pte. Luckee H. returned from leave. 2 mules 8/ 1 horse to IX Corps M.T.S.	

A.R.Smyth
Captain.
O.C., 3rd. Div. T.S.

Capt. A.R. Smyth
O.C. 31 M.V.S.

WAR DIARY
or
INTELLIGENCE SUMMARY.
(Erase heading not required.)

Army Form C. 2118.

Place	Date	Hour	Summary of Events and Information	Remarks and references to Appendices
LOCRE	Oct 1917 1		Routine work. Cpl Rothory to Hom. leave. 6954 Pte Grant & 1 Raw Flanders attach.	
	2		" 20 horses & 8 mules to 23 Vety Hosp.	
	3		" 1907 Pte Brown C to 877 Amb.	
	4		"	
	5		" 1 horse to 1x M.V.D.	
	6		"	
	7		" 1 horse & 1 mule to 1x M.V.D.	
	8		" 6439. Pte Whitfield on leave	
	9		" 12 horses & 12 mules to 23 Vety Hospital	
	10		"	
	11		" 6582 Pte Moore G on leave	
	12		" 2 mules & 1 horse to 1x M.V.D	
	13		" 1 mule to 1x M.V.D.	
	14		"	
	15		" 2 horses & 2 mules to 1x M.V.D. 10 horses & 5 mules to 23 Vety	
	16		Hosp. Sgr Howe. Cpl Daly. & Pte Tucker to 2 mvil Clipping Depot.	
	17		Routine work	
	18		" Staff Sergeant Murphy H. on leave	
	19		"	
	20		" 1 horse to 1x M.V.D.	

WAR DIARY
or
INTELLIGENCE SUMMARY.
(Erase heading not required.)

Army Form C. 2118.

Capt A R Smythe AVC Shula
O C 31 M.V.S

Place	Date 1917 Oct	Hour	Summary of Events and Information	Remarks and references to Appendices
LOCRE	21		Routine work. 6489 Pte Whitfield L returned from leave. Sgt. Briggs to Clipping Depot.	
	22		" . Sgt. Hime S returned. Picture from Clipping Depot.	
	23		" " 22 Iudw to Corps Dep. 11 Horses 8 mules to 23 H Hosp.	
	24		" " 6718 Pte Booth P on leave. 6582 Pte Moore J returned from leave. 6 horses	
	25		" 2 mules to 1X M.V.D	
	26		Routine work. 6527 Pte Tugwell R on leave.	
	27		" "	
	28		" "	
	29		" " 12 horses 1 mule to 23 Vety Hosp. Staff Sergt Supt. H returned	
	30		from leave. 25703 Pte Cartwright H reported for duty from 24HA. 6448 Cpl Darby F on leave.	
	31		Routine work. 8 horses & meets to 1X M.V.D	
			The weather has been generally cold & unsettled.	

A R Smythe AVC
Capt
O C 31 M Vet Sec

WAR DIARY or INTELLIGENCE SUMMARY

Capt. H.R. Smythe A.V.C. OC 31 M.V.S

Vol 28

Army Form C. 2118.

(Erase heading not required.)

Place	Date Nov 1917	Hour	Summary of Events and Information	Remarks and references to Appendices
LOCRE	1		Routine work.	
	2		1 horse to 1X M.V.O. – 1 horse returned from 1X M.V.O.	
	3		6144 Pte Perry R.R. on leave. 1 horse to 1X M.V.O.	
	4		6518 Pte Doty P. returned from leave.	
	5		S766 Sgt Howe.S. on leave. 670 Leng Dewsnubb W. A/C reported for duty from 19 Vety Hospital	
	6		28 horses & 4 mules to 23 V. Hosp. 21 mules to 1X Corps Dep	
	7		2 horses to 1X M.V.O.	
	8		9 1 mule to 1X M.V.O. – 6527 Pte Lugwell R. from leave – 6517 Pte Tracy on leave	
	9		Routine	
MERRIS	10		Moved to MERRIS	
	11		Routine. MERRIS bombed by hostile aircraft.	
	12		Moved to RACQUINHAM via HAZEBROUCK.	
RACQUINHAM	13		Routine	
	14		4 men attached for clipping	
	15		Routine & erection of shelters for horses	
	16		Routine	
	17		5298 Pte Allen returned to duty from Divl Clipping Depot.	

(Stub)

WAR DIARY
or
INTELLIGENCE SUMMARY.

Army Form C. 2118.

Capt/A.R Smyth AVC
OC 31 M.V.S.

(Erase heading not required.)

Instructions regarding War Diaries and Intelligence Summaries are contained in F. S. Regs., Part II. and the Staff Manual respectively. Title pages will be prepared in manuscript.

Place	Date	Hour	Summary of Events and Information	Remarks and references to Appendices
	18		8 Horses & Mules to 23 Veterinary Hospital.	
	19		No 6544 Pte Perry returned from leave (ADO Tx M.V.D)	
	20		Routine	
	21		6 Horses & Mules to 23 Veterinary Hospital. No 1766 Seng/Howes S returned from leave.	
	22		3201 Shoeing Smith Herron J.A. on 14 days leave.	
	24		Capt. A.R Smyth L. on leave. Command of Section turned over to Capt. S.S Kerr AVC. S/766 Seng/Howes S reverted to Corps & dispatches to No 10 Vety Hosp. (Authority A.A & U.S IX Corps. VB 287 c) 28.10.17)	
	25		Routine	
	26		Routine	
	27		2 Mules to 23 Veterinary Hospital.	
	28		Routine	
	29		Routine	
	30		7094. Pte Wynn L on leave.	
	31		The weather has been generally fair & cold. Occasional rains & windy from 25 to 29 x.	

S.S Kerr. Capt AVC

WAR DIARY
or
INTELLIGENCE SUMMARY.
(Erase heading not required.)

Army Form C. 2118.

Place	Date	Hour	Summary of Events and Information	Remarks and references to Appendices
Field (RACQUINCHEM)	1-12-17		7 horses evacuated to 23rd Vety Hospital	
	2.12.17		Routine	
	3.12.17		Routine	
	4.12.17		Routine	
	5.12.17		3 Horses & 3 mules evacuated to 23rd Vety Hospital & two hides 2.M.C.O. 91. Man rejoined from Divisional Clipping Depot 1.M.C. 093mm rejoined from IV Corps. M.V.D.	
	6.12.17		Routine	
	7.12.17		1 Horse evacuated to 23rd Vety Hospital, entrained at ST. OMER	
	8.12.17		Detrained at MONDICOURT 2 a.m. & marched to ACHIET-LE-PETIT via BASSEAUX.	
ACHIET. LE PETIT O.36.c.57	9 - 12.17		In Camp at ACHIET. LE. PETIT	
	10-12.17		Marched to O.36.C.5.7 Sheet 57c.	
	11.12.17		In Camp. no 3201 P.S. Herron H. returned from leave to England.	
	12.12.17		No 23470 Pte Mitchell R. proceeded on leave to Paisy le Grange (P+O) (14 Days) from 13-12-17 to 27-12-17. Capt Smythe a.v.c. returned from leave to England.	

MOBILE VETERINARY SECTION 31ST

Army Form C. 2118.

WAR DIARY
or
INTELLIGENCE SUMMARY.
(Erase heading not required.)

Instructions regarding War Diaries and Intelligence Summaries are contained in F. S. Regs., Part II. and the Staff Manual respectively. Title pages will be prepared in manuscript.

2

Place	Date	Hour	Summary of Events and Information	Remarks and references to Appendices
O3 Field	13-12-17		Routine	
MANANCOURT	14-12-17		Marched to MANANCOURT, 1 R.C.O 93 men proceeded to join No 5 C.C.S.	
	15-12-17		Routine	
NEUVILLE	16-12-17		Section marched to NEUVILLE area, No 7074 Pte Flynn J. returned from leave to England.	
	17-12-17		Routine	
	18-12-17		Routine	
	19-12-17		Routine	
	20-12-17		5 Horses & 3 Mules evacuated to No 5 C.C.S.	
	21-12-17		Routine	
	22-12-17		No 9913 Pte Potter W.J. wounded by Bomb.	
	23-12-17		No 9913 Pte Potter W.J. died from wounds at No 21 C.C.S.	
			15 Horses & 4 Mules evacuated to No 5 C.C.S.	
	24-12-17		Moved into Billets at NEUVILLE	
	25-12-17		17 Horses evacuated to No 5 C.C.S.	
	26-12-17		10 Horses evacuated to No 5 C.C.S.	

31ST MOBILE VETERINARY SECTION

Army Form C. 2118.

WAR DIARY
or
INTELLIGENCE SUMMARY.

(Erase heading not required.)

3

Place	Date	Hour	Summary of Events and Information	Remarks and references to Appendices
Field (NEUVILLE)	27.12.17		33 Horses evacuated to No 5 C.C.S.	
	28.12.17		4 Horses & 1 Mule evacuated to No 5 C.C.S. No 23470 Pte Mitchell R. returned from leave.	
	29.12.17		19 Horses evacuated to No 5 C.C.S.	
	30.12.17		12 Horses evacuated to No 5 C.C.S.	
	31.12.17		9 Horses evacuated to No 5 C.C.S.	

31ST
MOBILE VETERINARY
SECTION.
No.............
Date............

31st Mob. Vet. Sec.

WAR DIARY
or
INTELLIGENCE SUMMARY.
(Erase heading not required.)

Army Form C. 2118.

JANUARY

Place	Date	Hour	Summary of Events and Information	Remarks and references to Appendices
NEUVILLE	1/1/18	—	15,, Horses,, Evacuated To. 5, C.C.S.	
,,	2/1/18	—	14,, Horses,, — — To 5, C.C.S,, 627,, Sergt Robson J.W. Joined for Duty from 14, Vet. Hosp.	
,,	3/1/18	—	10,, Horses. 1 Mule — To 5, C.C.S	
,,	4/1/18	—	4,, Horses 2 Mules — To 5, C.C.S	
,,	5/1/18	—	7,, Horses — — To 5, C.C.S	
,,	6/1/18	—	9,, Horses 1 Mule — To 5, C.C.S SE/1907,, Pte Brown.C. Joined for Duty from No 2 Vet Hosp.	
,,	7/1/18	—	6,, Horses 2 Mules - To 5, C.C.S.	
,,	8/1/18	—	Routine Work,,	
,,	9/1/18	—	12,, Horses Evacuated,To, 5, C.C.S,	
,,	10/1/18	—	8,, Horses — — To, 5, C.C.S.	
,,	11/1/18	—	5,, Horses 2 Mules - To, 5 C.C.S	
,,	12/1/18	—	7,, Horses — — To.5 C.C.S.	
,,	13/1/18	—	8,, Horses — — To. 5. C.C.S. 9354 Cowley R. Pte Leave To England From 15/1/18 to 30/1/18	
,,	14/1/18	—	Routine Work,,	
,,	15/1/18	—	Routine Work,, — — — 4030. Sergt Briggs S. Leave To England From 14/1/18 to 1/2/18	
,,	16/1/18	—	Routine Work,,	

A.F. Hunt Capt. A.V.C.
O/C 31st Mobile Vet. Section
31/1/18

JANUARY
WAR DIARY
or
INTELLIGENCE SUMMARY.
(Erase heading not required.)

Army Form C. 2118.

Place	Date	Hour	Summary of Events and Information	Remarks and references to Appendices
NEUVILLE	17/1/18	/	9 Horses 3 Mules Evacuated To 5 C.C.S.	
"	18/1/18	/	4 Horses 1 Mule — — — To 5 C.C.S. 4/10916 Gunner Ashcroft S. 24254 Dr Garwood W. A.F.A. Attached For Duty 31st M.V.S 298/3/2	
"	19/1/18	/	Routine	
"	20/1/18	/	15 Horses — — — — To 5 C.C.S. 13299 Pte Fiddler, Leave To England 22/1/18 To 6/2/18	
"	21/1/18	/	Routine	
"	22/1/18	/	12 Horses 5 Mules — — To 5 C.C.S. Gunner Ashcroft. S. Dr Garwood W. To 5 C.C.S Transferred	
"	23/1/18	/	Routine	
"	24/1/18	/	1 Mule — — To 5 C.C.S	
"	25/1/18	/	6 Horses — — — — To 5 C.C.S	
"	26/1/18	/	11 Horses 8 Mules — — To 5 C.C.S. 984 Pte Heath A.J. Leave To England 28/1/18 To 11/2/18	
"	27/1/18	/	1 Horse — — — — To 5 C.C.S.	
"	28/1/18	/	6 Horses 2 Mules — To 5 C.C.S.	
"	29/1/18	/	2 Horses — — — — To 5 C.C.S.	
"	30/1/18	/	Routine	
"	31/1/18	/	6 Horses 2 Mules — To 5 C.C.S 11478 A/Cpl Boyle Leave To England 2/2/18 To 16/2/18	

A.S. Murphy Capt. A.V.C.
O/C 31st Mobile Vet-Section 31/1/18

Army Form C. 2118.

WAR DIARY
or
INTELLIGENCE SUMMARY

31 Mob. Vety Sec 1920

Vol 31

(Erase heading not required.)

Place	Date	Hour	Summary of Events and Information	Remarks and references to Appendices
NEUVILLE	1/2/18		Routine	
	2/2/18		5 Horses & 2 Mules evacuated to No 5. C.C.S.	
	3/2/18		No 9357. Pte Early R. A.V.C. returned from leave to United Kingdom	
	4/2/18		6 Horses evacuated to No 5 C.C.S.	
			No 4030. A/Sgt. Buggs J. A.V.C. returned from leave to United Kingdom	
	5/2/18		4 Horses & 2 Mules evacuated to No 5 C.C.S.	
	6/2/18		Routine	
	7/2/18		No 627. A/Sgt. Robson D.W. A.V.C. proceed on leave to United Kingdom Period 8/2/18 to 22/2/18 via Boulogne.	
			No 37197. Pte Clegg J. W. 7th Batt. South Lancs. Regt & two Horses Temporarily attached	
	8/2/18		No 13299. Pte Fidler E. 7th Batt. Loyal North Lancs returned from leave to United Kingdom	
			No 13299. Pte. Fidler E. 7th Batt. L.N.Lancs rejoined his regiment on Completion of Course of Draining (Veterinary)	

2449 Wt. W14957/M90 750,600 1/16 J.B.C. & A. Forms/C.2118/12.

Army Form C. 2118.

WAR DIARY
or
INTELLIGENCE SUMMARY

(Erase heading not required.)

Place	Date	Hour	Summary of Events and Information	Remarks and references to Appendices
NEUVILLE	10/2/18		Routine	
	11/2/18		3 Horses evacuated to No 5 C.C.S.	
	12/2/18		Routine	
	13/2/18		No. 787 S/S Pte Heath A. A.V.C. returned from leave to United Kingdom. 7 Horses & 2 Mules evacuated to No 5 C.C.S.	
	14/2/18		2 Horses evacuated to No 5 C.C.S.	
LE MESNIL	15/2/18		Section marched to Le Mesnil. U.A.B. 84. Sheet 57c. No. 25481 Pte Metcalfe A. A.V.C. Proceeded on leave to United Kingdom period 16/2/18 to 2/3/18. via Boulogne. No 37197. Pte Clegg. J.W. 7th Batt South Lancs & 2 Horses returned to unit	
	16/2/18		No 48029. Dr Langton A. R.F.A attached for rations & discipline (Temporarily) No. 41668. Sergt. Henry. O. 9th Cheshire Regt. Temporarily attached as Musketry Instructor.	
	17/2/18		No 9357 S/S Pte Early R. A.V.C. Transferred (Temporarily) for duty to M.V.D 3rd Army	

Army Form C. 2118.

WAR DIARY
or
INTELLIGENCE SUMMARY

(Erase heading not required.)

VII

Place	Date	Hour	Summary of Events and Information	Remarks and references to Appendices
LE MESNIL	18/2/18		Routine	
	19/2/18		No 11478 Se/Pte Castle. E. A.O.C. returned from leave to United Kingdom	
			11 Horses & 2 Mules evacuated to No 5 C.C.S.	
	20/2/18		No 1907. Se/Pte Brown. C. A.O.C. proceeded on leave to United Kingdom period 21/2/18 to 7/3/18. Via Boulogne.	
			No. 2027. Dr Langton. A. R.F.A returned to unit.	
			No 10022 Pte Preston. P. 15th Batt. James Fusiliers, attached 19th D.H.Q. Temporarily attached for rations & discipline	
			6 Horses evacuated to No 5 C.C.S.	
	21/2/18		No 1668 Sergt. Henry. O. 9th Batt. Cheshire Regt. evacuated sick	
			5 Horses & 1 Mule evacuated to No 5 C.C.S.	
	22/2/18		Routine	
	23/2/18		Routine	
	24/2/18		Routine	
	25/2/18		No 25703. Pte Cartwright. N.W. are leave to United Kingdom Period 26/2/18 to 12/3/18 via Boulogne	
			No 10022 Pte Preston P. 15th Batt. James Fus. returned to unit, 7 Horses evacuated to No 5 C.C.S.	

Army Form C. 2118.

WAR DIARY
or
INTELLIGENCE SUMMARY

(Erase heading not required.)

Instructions regarding War Diaries and Intelligence Summaries are contained in F. S. Regs., Part II. and the Staff Manual respectively. Title Pages will be prepared in manuscript.

IV

Place	Date	Hour	Summary of Events and Information	Remarks and references to Appendices
LE MEGNIL	26/2/18		No 16540. Pte Marsden. A. 10th Batt Worcester Regt. Temporarily attached for rations & discipline	
	27/2/18		3 Horses & 2 Mules evacuated to No 5 C.C.S.	
	28/2/18		Routine	

31st
MOBILE VETERINARY
SECTION.

No....
Date

A.F. Dunlop Capt. R.A.V.C.
O.C. 31st M.V. Sec.
31st M.V.S.

WAR DIARY or INTELLIGENCE SUMMARY

Army Form C. 2118.

31 Mob Vety Sec 19

Place	Date	Hour	Summary of Events and Information	Remarks and references to Appendices
LE MESNIL	1-3-18		Routine Work. No T4/144833 Dr BRIDGEWATER O. A.S.C att 31st M.V.S. proceeded on leave to UNITED KINGDOM. Passed 2/3/18 to 16/3/18 via BOULOGNE	
	2-3-18		4 HORSES evacuated to No 6 C.C.S.	
	3-3-18		Routine Work.	
	4-3-18		4 HORSES & 2 MULES evacuated to No 6 C.C.S. No 25481 Pte METCALFE. A. Returned from leave to UNITED KINGDOM	
	5-3-18		Routine Work. No SE/1774 Pte BROWN. G. Evacuated Sick to 67th FIELD AMBULANCE	
	6-3-18		6 HORSES Evacuated to No 6 C.C.S. No SE/6399 Pte HUME R. Proceeded on leave to UNITED KINGDOM Passed 6-3-18 to 20-3-18 via BOULOGNE	

WAR DIARY
or
INTELLIGENCE SUMMARY (2)

(Erase heading not required.)

Army Form C. 2118.

Instructions regarding War Diaries and Intelligence Summaries are contained in F. S. Regs., Part II. and the Staff Manual respectively. Title Pages will be prepared in manuscript.

Place	Date	Hour	Summary of Events and Information	Remarks and references to Appendices
Le Maisnil	7-3-18		Routine Work.	
	8-3-18		Routine Work.	
	9-3-18		9 Horses & 2 Mules evacuated to No 5 C.C.S. No 54/907 Pte Brown.C. returned from leave to United Kingdom	
	10-3-18		Routine Work.	
	11-3-18		Routine Work.	
	12-3-18		6 Horses evacuated to No 5 C.C.S.	
	13-3-18		Routine Work.	
	14-3-18		Routine Work. No 14371H Pte Faiers. W.C. 290th Employment Coy. Attached for return & discipline	
	15-3-18		8 Horses & 3 Mules evacuated to No 5 C.C.S.	
	16-3-18		Routine Work. No 25703 Pte Cartwright. H.W. returned from	
	17-3-18		Routine Work. Leave to United Kingdom.	
	18-3-18		11 Horses & 1 Mule evacuated to No 5 C.C.S. No 74/144233 Dvr Bridgewater. O. A.S.C. returned from leave to United Kingdom.	
	19-3-18		No 203266 Pte Davis. T. 6th Batt Wilts Regt attached for return & discipline	

Army Form C. 2118.

WAR DIARY
or
INTELLIGENCE SUMMARY. (3)
(Erase heading not required.)

Instructions regarding War Diaries and Intelligence Summaries are contained in F. S. Regs., Part II. and the Staff Manual respectively. Title pages will be prepared in manuscript.

Place	Date	Hour	Summary of Events and Information	Remarks and references to Appendices
LE MESNIL	20.3.18		Routine Work.	
	21.3.18		4 Horses & 6 Mules evacuated to N⁰ 6 C.C.S.	
	22.3.18		N⁰ 22579 Pte BAKER. J.R.	
			" 21796 " BUTCHER. L.S. } Joined for duty from N⁰ 14 V Itinerary	
			" 9948 " BOUGH. E. Hospital for duty with 31ˢᵗ M.V.S.	
			" 22798 " CLAYTON. J.E.	
			" 19980 " CORBEY. J.H.	
			" 26727 " DALLIMORE. H.	
			" 20093 " FRASER. T.	
			" 20039 " HARDING. F.	
	23.3.18		Section marched to L.E. TRANSLOY. Halted 2 Hours. Then marched to JRLES. arrived 3am 24.3.18, rested 7 hours, then marched to BUCQUOY.	
BUCQUOY	24.3.18		Section in Camp at BUCQUOY.	
HENU	25.3.18		Section marched to HENU.	
MONDICOURT	26.3.18		Section marched to MONDICOURT. N⁰ 9945 Pte BOUCH. E. missing	
	27.3.18		Section in Camp at MONDICOURT.	

Army Form C. 2118.

WAR DIARY
or
INTELLIGENCE SUMMARY. (4)

(Erase heading not required.)

Instructions regarding War Diaries and Intelligence Summaries are contained in F. S. Regs., Part II. and the Staff Manual respectively. Title pages will be prepared in manuscript.

Place	Date	Hour	Summary of Events and Information	Remarks and references to Appendices
MONDICOURT	28.3.18		16 HORSES & 5 MULES evacuated to 14 Veterinary Hospital	
	29.3.18		Return in Camp at MONDICOURT.	
	30.3.18		Section marched to CANDAS. entrained at 5 P.M. for CAISTRE. arrived at 2.45 A.M. 31-3-18. detrained & marched to DRANOUTRE	
DRANOUTRE	31.3.18		In Billets at DRANOUTRE M.35.A.4.2. Sheet 28	

31ST
MOBILE VETERINARY
SECTION.

R. Hunt Capt. R.V.C.
O.C. 31 M.V. Sec.

Army Form C. 2118.

31 Inf Bde See
Vol 31

WAR DIARY
or
INTELLIGENCE SUMMARY.
(Erase heading not required.)

Instructions regarding War Diaries and Intelligence Summaries are contained in F. S. Regs., Part II. and the Staff Manual respectively. Title pages will be prepared in manuscript.

Place	Date	Hour	Summary of Events and Information	Remarks and references to Appendices
DRANOUTRE	1/4/18		Routine No 1679 Pte BUTLER. A. 6th Royal Irish Regr. temporarily attached for rations & quartered	
"	2/4/18		Routine.	
NIEPPE	3/4/18		Section marched to B.8 & 5.7. Met 36 Nieppe. The following N.C.O & men transferred to No 2 Stay Hospital temporarily subject to Medical Inspection re transfer re infantry. Authority D.V.S. 2/258/18, dated 13/3/18.	
			No 6438 Cpl Darby J.	
			" 11478 Pte Lovett H.	
			" 6339 " Hunt R.	
			" 25481 " Metcalfe A. } 31st M.V.S	
			" 23470 " Mitchell Ry.	
			" 6527 " Tugwell R.	
			" 6439 " Wilkie A.	
			The following N.C.O & men temporarily attached for rations & discipline:-	
			No 374543 L/Cpl Hdr G. } 754th Area Employment Coy.	
			" 374529 Pte Dick. A.	
			" 32694 " Thistle G. } 83rd Area Employment Coy.	
			" 470693 " Dean. M.S.	
NIEPPE	4/4/18		Routine.	
"	5/4/18		25 Horses & 7 Mules evacuated by barge to 23 Stat. Hospital.	
			No 5228 Pte Otter.W. rejoined from leave to England. The following men rejoined from No 5. L.L.S.	
			No 787 Pte Heath.A.	
			" 1593 " Mitchell. F.	
			" 6524 " Perry J.R.	
			The following man rejoined from No 3 Employment Depot.	
			No 6945 Pte Boucher E.	

Army Form C. 2118.

WAR DIARY
or
INTELLIGENCE SUMMARY.
(Erase heading not required.)

(2.)

Instructions regarding War Diaries and Intelligence Summaries are contained in F.S. Regs., Part II. and the Staff Manual respectively. Title pages will be prepared in manuscript.

Place	Date	Hour	Summary of Events and Information	Remarks and references to Appendices
NIEPPE	5/4/18		The following men joined for duty from No 15 Vety Hospital :- No 14469 Pte HAMPTON.R. " 22606 " WILLIAMS.G.J. } A.V.C.	
"	6/4/18		Routine	
"	7/4/18		No. 1369 Pte NEWMAN.W. 6th Wilts. Temporarily attached for rations & discipline. " 203266 " DAVIS.T. 6th Wilts. Returned to his unit permanently. Received new horse ambulance.	
"	8/4/18		No. 13502 Pte NORTON.J. 9th WELSH Temporarily attached for rations & discipline. " 1573 " MITCHELL.F. A.V.C. Transferred to No.2. Vety. Hospital temporarily subject to Medical Inspection on transfer to infantry. auth. D.V.S 2/258/18 dated 13/3/18	
"	9/4/18		No. 13502 Pte NORTON J 9th WELSH " 143714 " FAIERS.W.C. 19th DIV. EMPLOYMENT COY.} transferred to 19th D.H.Q. permanently.	
"	10/4/18		Section marched out of billets 12.30 a.m. to LA CRECHE. Rested for 6 hours. Marched to CROIX DE POPERINGHE M.32.B. Sheet 28.	
CROIX DE POPERINGHE	11/4/18		In billets. Routine	
"	12/4/18		Section marched at 2.a.m. to L.29.B. Central. BOESCHEPE. Sheet 27. 22 horses & 7 mules to 22nd V.E.S. The following N.C.O. & men transferred to 22nd V.E.S. temporarily for duty :-	
BOESCHEPE			No. 637 Sgt. ROBSON.D.W. " 9945 Pte. BOUCH.E " 26727 " DALLIMORE.H. } A.V.C. " 7074 " FLYNN.J. " 25703 " CARTWRIGHT.H.W. " 14469 " HAMPTON.R.	

Army Form C. 2118.

WAR DIARY
or
INTELLIGENCE SUMMARY.
(Erase heading not required.)

(3).

Place	Date	Hour	Summary of Events and Information	Remarks and references to Appendices
L.29. A.S.C.M.T.R.D.	13/4/18		No. 16219 PTE M.I.+S. & 9th WELSH. Transferred to 19th D.H.Q. Permanently for duty. Section marched at 6 P.M. to L.29.A Central Shut 27 Encamped in tents.	
"	14/4/18		Section in camp. Routine work.	
"	15/4/18		Routine work.	
"	16/4/18		Routine No. 165140 PTE. MARSDEN. A. 10th WORCESTER Regt returned to his unit for duty permanently.	
ABEELE	17/4/18		Section marched at 5 p.m. to L.31.A.3.8. Sheet 27. ABEELE. 9 horses + 4 mules evacuated to 23 VETY. HOSPITAL.	
"	18/4/18		Section in camp. Routine work.	
"	19/4/18		3 horses & 1 mule to 23 M.V.E.S. The following N.C.O & men rejoined from No.2 VETY. HOSPITAL having been rejected by Medical Board as unfit for infantry:-	
"	20/4/18		No. 6458 Cpl DARLEY. F " 6339 Pte HUME. R. " 25481 " METCALFE. A. " 23470 " MITCHELL. R.W. } A.V.C. " 6527 " TUGWELL. R. " 6439 " WHITFIELD. A. The following man rejoined from M.V.D. 3rd ARMY. No. 9357 Pte EARLEY. R.	
PROVEN	21/4/18		Section marched at 9 a.m. to E.12 located Sheet 27. Encamped for the night.	
"	22/4/18		Section in camp Routine work.	

Army Form C. 2118.

WAR DIARY
or
INTELLIGENCE SUMMARY.
(Erase heading not required.)

(4.)

Place	Date	Hour	Summary of Events and Information	Remarks and references to Appendices
GODEWAERSVELDE	23/4/18		Section marched at 9 p.m. to GODEWAERSVELDE. Q.18.A.3.8. Sheet 27. 8 horses evacuated to 2nd CORPS V.E.S. The following O.R's rejoined from 22nd V.E.S. :- No. 25703 Pte CARTWRIGHT, H.W. } A.V.C. " 14469 " HAMPTON. R.	
"	24/4/18		Section in camp. Routine work.	
"	25/4/18		The following O.R's transferred to 22nd V.E.S. temporarily for duty :- No. 19980 Pte CORBEY, J.H. } A.V.C. " 6339 " HUME. R.	
"	26/4/18		The following O.R's transferred to No 2 VETY. HOSPITAL permanently :- No. 25703 Pte CARTWRIGHT H.W. " 14469 " HAMPTON. R. " 20039 " HARDING. F. } A.V.C. " 25481 " METCALFE. A. " 23470 " MITCHELL. R.W. " 22606 " WILLIAMS. O.J. Section marched out of billets 4 p.m. to Q.6.c.2.9. Sheet 27.	
"	27/4/18 28/4/18 29/4/18		Section in camp. Routine work. 3 horses & 3 mules evacuated to 8th CORPS V.E.S. Routine work.	
"	30/4/18		Routine work.	

J. W. [signature]
Capt. A.V.C.
O.C. 51st Mob. Vet. Sec.

51st MOBILE VETERINARY SECTION.

19

31 M Vet Sec

Vol 34 Sheet 1

Army Form C. 2118.

WAR DIARY
or
INTELLIGENCE SUMMARY.
(Erase heading not required.)

Instructions regarding War Diaries and Intelligence Summaries are contained in F. S. Regs., Part II. and the Staff Manual respectively. Title pages will be prepared in manuscript.

Place	Date	Hour	Summary of Events and Information	Remarks and references to Appendices
GODEWAERSVELDE	1.5.18		In Camp. Six horses evacuated to No 8 V.E.S. Routine Work.	
"	2.5.18		Routine Work.	
"	3.5.18		Six horses & two mules evacuated to No 8. V.E.S.	
"	4.5.18		Marched our H camp at 10 a.m. to K.30.a.bb. Shew 27. Two horses & one mule killed & nine horses wounded by well fire.	
K30 a.b.b. Shew 27	5.5.18		Eight horses & three mules to 32nd V.E.S. No 1364 PTE NEWMAN W. 1st WILTS transferred to 22nd V.E.S. with horse (wounded) belonging to Colonel Lord A Thynne.	
"	6.5.18		In Camp. Routine Work.	
"	7.5.18		Eight horses evacuated to 22nd V.E.S.	
"	8.5.18		Routine Work. In Camp.	
"	9.5.18		Two horses & one mule evacuated to 22nd V.E.S. One Mule reg No 25 H 22nd V.E.S.	
"	10.5.18		One horse evacuated to 22nd V.E.S. No 637 Sgt ROBSON.D.W. transferred One horse & one mule evacuated to No 2 VETERINARY HOSPITAL.	
"	11.5.18		Remained for duty from 22nd V.E.S. to No 2 VETERINARY HOSPITAL. Routine work. In Camp.	
"	12.5.18		Routine Work. In Camp.	
"	13.5.18		Five horses & one mule evacuated to 22nd V.E.S.	
"	14.5.18		One horse & one mule evacuated to 22nd V.E.S.	
"	15.5.18		In Camp. Routine Work.	
"	16.5.18		Two horses evacuated to 22nd V.E.S.	
"	17.5.18	8.30am 4.50pm	Section marched to WAAVENBERG for entraining. Train departed.	
ON TRAIN	18.5.18		En Route.	
CHEPY	19.5.18	5.15am	Section arrived at Railhead & proceeded by tram/marched to billet at CHEPY.	
"	20.5.18		In Camp. Routine work. A	
"	21.5.18		Routine Work.	

Army Form C. 2118.

Sheet. 2.

WAR DIARY
or
INTELLIGENCE SUMMARY.
(Erase heading not required.)

Instructions regarding War Diaries and Intelligence Summaries are contained in F. S. Regs., Part II. and the Staff Manual respectively. Title pages will be prepared in manuscript.

Place	Date	Hour	Summary of Events and Information	Remarks and references to Appendices
CHEPY	22.5.18		In Camp. Routine M&K.	
"	23.5.18		In Camp. Routine Thops.	
"	24.5.18		In Camp. Routine Work.	
"	25.5.18		In Camp. Routine Work.	
"	26.5.18		In Camp. Routine Work.	
"	27.5.18		In Camp. Routine M&K.	
"	28.5.18 10.50am		Section marched to AIGNY arriving at 6pm Encamped for night	
AIGNY	29.5.18 8.30am		Section marched through VENTEUIL and halted by the road for night	
VENTEUIL	30.5.18 7am		Sectn marched to MAUFAUX. Encamped for the night.	
MAUFAUX	31.5.18 7am		Sectn marched to NANTEUIL. Encamped for the night.	

[signature]
Capt. A.V.C.
O.C. 31st Mobile Vety Section

[Stamp: 31st MOBILE VETERINARY SECTION]

Army Form C. 2118.

WAR DIARY
or
INTELLIGENCE SUMMARY.
(Erase heading not required.)

Sheet 1

Place	Date	Hour	Summary of Events and Information	Remarks and references to Appendices
NANTEUIL	1/6/18		Section in camp	
"	2/6/18		Section marched at 1.a.m. to DIZY-MAGENTA, arriving at 4.30 a.m.	
PIERRY	3/6/18		Section marched at 12.15 a.m to PIERRY - Rifle Range.	
"	4/6/18		In camp. Routine work.	
"	5/6/18		In camp. Routine work.	
"	6/6/18		In camp. Routine work	
"	7/6/18		In camp. Routine work.	
"	8/6/18		In camp. Routine work. No 10070 Pte POUNTLEY.W. 9th CHESHIRES: No 20017 Pte GROVES.B.G. 1/4th K.S.L.I: No 15024 Pte HARRISON.E. 8th N.STAFFS: No 9572 Pte HOLLINS.H. 10th WORCESTERS: No 44667 Pte BONIFACE.R.D. 8th GLDSTERS: No 21198 Pte KERLEY.B.A. 10th WARWICKS: No 11245 Pte VESEY.H. 6th WILTS: No 63080 Pte JAMES.C.H. 9th WELSH: No 54246 Pte THOMAS.R. 9th P.W.F.S: attached for temporary duty.	
"	9/6/18		No 1679 Pte BUTLER.A. 6th ROYAL IRISH REGT, returned to 19th D.H.Q. for duty	

Army Form C. 2118.

WAR DIARY
or
INTELLIGENCE SUMMARY.
(Erase heading not required.)

JUNE 1918 Sheet 2

Place	Date	Hour	Summary of Events and Information	Remarks and references to Appendices
PIERRY	10/6/18		25 horses & one mule evacuated to No 9 V.E.S. No 5228 Pte ATTER W transferred to No 2 VETERINARY HOSPITAL. Being surplus to Establishment. 4 Horses sold to Butchers at EPERNAY.	
"	11/6/18		3 horses evacuated to No 9 V.E.S. 1 horse sold to Butchers at EPERNAY.	
"	12/6/18		Routine in camp.	
"	13/6/18		10 horses & 3 mules evacuated to No 9 V.E.S.	
"	14/6/18		Routine in camp.	
"	15/6/18		Routine in camp.	
"	16/6/18		6 horses & 3 mules evacuated to No 9 V.E.S. No 393 S. Sgt JUPP H.T. transferred to No 7 VETERINARY HOSPITAL. Authority D.V.S. 2/1286/18 dated 26/5/18.	
"	17/6/18		Routine in camp.	

Army Form C. 2118.

WAR DIARY
or
INTELLIGENCE SUMMARY.
(Erase heading not required.)

JUNE 1918   Sheet 3

Place	Date	Hour	Summary of Events and Information	Remarks and references to Appendices
PIERRY	18/6/18		No 21198 Pte KERLEY.B.A. 10th WARWICKS: No 9375 Pte HOLLINS.H. 10th WORCESTERS: No 63080 Pte JAMES.C.H. O/X WELSH: No 51016 Pte THOMAS.R. 9x R.W.F.S. returned to their units.	
"	19/6/18		No 20093 Pte FRASER.T. evacuated sick through 58th FIELD AMB. to C.C.S.	
"	20/6/18		Section marched at 4pm to LE MESNIL-sur-OGER arriving at 3.15pm Billeted for the night	
LE MESNIL sur OGER	21/6/18		Section marched at 9.30 a.m. to REUVES - MONDEMONT road, just outside the former village.	
REUVES	22/6/18		In Camp. No 15090 Pte POUNTLEY.W 9th CHESHIRES: No 200471 Pte GROVES.B.G. 14th K.S.L.I. No 15024 Pte HARRISON.G. 8th N.STAFFS: No 44667 Pte BONIFACE.R.D. 8th GLOSTERS: No 11245 Pte VESEY.A. 6th WILTS. returned to their units.	
"	23/6/18		No 63080 Pte JAMES.C.H. O/X WELSH: attached for temporary duty. No 6541 CPL.TUCKER.H. evacuated sick through 57th FIELD AMB. to C.C.S.	
"	24/6/18		No 627 SGT. ROBSON.D.W. reported to section for duty from 10th DIVISIONAL WING REINFORCEMENT CAMP.	
"	25/6/18		Section marched at 10.30 a.m. to 1/2 Kilom. North of the S in BANNES. (Map ref. CHALONS Sheet 50.) No 15024 Pte HARRISON.G. 8th N.STAFFS. rejoined section for temporary duty.	

Army Form C. 2118.

WAR DIARY
or
INTELLIGENCE SUMMARY.
(Erase heading not required.)

JUNE 1918

Place	Date	Hour	Summary of Events and Information	Remarks and references to Appendices
BANNES	26/6/18		No 438911 Sapper OKE.A.P. 81st R.E.S. attached for temporary duty. 11 horses & 1 mule evacuated to No 9 V.E.S.	
"	27/6/18		No 4572 Pte LANG.G. 14th M.G. Battn. attached for temporary duty.	
"	28/6/18		4 horses & 2 mules evacuated to No 9 V.E.S. No 20093 Pte FRASER.T. from 19th DIVISIONAL WING REINFORCEMENT CAMP. 2 H.D. Remounts from No 9 V.E.S. for reissue. Issued to 12th M.G. Battn.	
"	29/6/18		Routine work.	
"	30/6/18		Routine work.	

Army Form C. 2118.

WAR DIARY
or
INTELLIGENCE SUMMARY.
(Erase heading not required.)

SHEET 1

Place	Date	Hour	Summary of Events and Information	Remarks and references to Appendices
BANNES	1/7/18		In camp ½ Kilometre NORTH of the S in BANNES. Section marched at 5.30pm to FERE-CHAMPENOISE	
FERE-CHAMPENOISE	2/7/18		Entrained at 6.30 am. Left at 8am.	
MARESQUEL	3/7/18		Detrained at 11am. at MARESQUEL. Section marched to BOURTHES arriving at 8pm.	
BOURTHES	4/7/18		In billets. Routine work.	
"	5/7/18		In billets. Routine work.	
"	6/7/18		In billets. Routine work.	
"	7/7/18		In billets. Routine work.	
"			Section marched at 9.a.m to FAUQUEMBERGUES, BOUT-DE-LA-VILLE arriving at 1.30pm. No 63080 Pte JAMES C.H. rejoined his unit 9th WELSH. No T.T. 03720 Pte ABBOTT A. A.V.C and No T.T. 02815 Pte SMITH W. joined the Section for duty from No 2 VETERINARY HOSPITAL.	
MILL S, of BOUT-DE-LA-VILLE	8/7/18		In camp. Routine work.	
"	9/7/18		No 15024 Pte HARRISON G. returned to 9th N.STAFFS. for duty	
"	10/7/18		No 4572 Pte LANG G. returned to 10th M.G. BATTN. for duty No T.T. 03877 Pte LOAT G. A.V.C. joined Section from A/84 BDE. R.F.A. for Upkeep to BASE	

Army Form C. 2118.

WAR DIARY
or
INTELLIGENCE SUMMARY.

(Erase heading not required.)

SHEET 2

Instructions regarding War Diaries and Intelligence Summaries are contained in F. S. Regs., Part II. and the Staff Manual respectively. Title pages will be prepared in manuscript.

Place	Date	Hour	Summary of Events and Information	Remarks and references to Appendices
MILL S.M. BOUT-DE-LA-VILLE	11/7/18		No 65244 Pte PERRY. J.R. to No 2 VETERINARY HOSPITAL being surplus to Establishment. No TT O387 Pte LOAT G. A.V.C. to No 2 VETERINARY HOSPITAL. Authority:- A.G.3.9/air TT/375/18 dated 1/7/18.	
"	12/7/18		In camp. Routine Work.	
"	13/7/18		Section marched at 7am. to BELLERY on the FERFAY ROAD arriving at 2pm. No 15338 Pte MAINE A. 3rd WORCESTER REGT. joined Section for temporary duty, rations and discipline.	
BELLERY	14/7/18		In billets. Routine Work.	
"	15/7/18		Eight horses & One mule evacuated to No XII VETERINARY EVACUATING STATION	
"	16/7/18		Routine Work	
"	17/7/18		No 3201 Sh. Smith HERRON. G.A. admitted to hospital sick via 57th FIELD AMBULANCE to C.R.S.	
"	18/7/18		Routine Work.	
"	19/7/18		Routine Work.	
"	20/7/18		Six horses & two mules to No XIII VETERINARY EVACUATING STATION.	
"	21/7/18		Routine Work.	

Army Form C. 2118.

SHEET 3

WAR DIARY
or
INTELLIGENCE SUMMARY.
(Erase heading not required.)

Instructions regarding War Diaries and Intelligence Summaries are contained in F. S. Regs., Part II. and the Staff Manual respectively. Title pages will be prepared in manuscript.

Place	Date	Hour	Summary of Events and Information	Remarks and references to Appendices
BELLEU	22/7/18		In Billets. Routine Work	
"	23/7/18		Routine Work	
"	24/7/18		Routine Work	
"	25/7/18		Routine Work	
"	26/7/18		Routine Work	
"	27/7/18		No 32201 Sho/Smith HERRON. G.A. A.V.C. returned from 30th CASUALTY CLEARING STATION	
"	28/7/18		Thirteen Horses & one mule evacuated to No XIII VETERINARY EVACUATING STATION	
"	29/7/18		Routine Work	
"	30/7/18		Fourteen horses & one mule evacuated to No XIII VETERINARY EVACUATING STATION	
"	31/7/18		Three horses & three mules evacuated to No XIII VETERINARY EVACUATING STATION	

31ST
MOBILE VETERINARY SECTION.
No.
Date 3/8/18

Army Form C. 2118.

31 Mob Vety Sec
Vol 37

WAR DIARY
or
INTELLIGENCE SUMMARY.
(Erase heading not required.)

Place	Date	Hour	Summary of Events and Information	Remarks and references to Appendices
BELLERY	1/8/18		Section in billets. One horse & one mule evacuated to No XIII VETERINARY EVACUATING STATION.	
"	2/8/18		In billets. Routine work.	
"	3/8/18		In billets. Routine work.	
"	4/8/18		In billets. Routine work.	
"	5/8/18		Three horses evacuated to No XIII VETERINARY EVACUATING STATION.	
"	6/8/18		Two horses & one mule evacuated to No VII VETERINARY EVACUATING STATION, and one horse to butchers. Section moved at 3pm to LAPUGNOY D.19.d.4.5. Bivouacked for the night.	
LAPUGNOY (Pop. d.4.5.) (Sheet 44B)	7/8/18		Section moved at 2.30pm to BOIS-DES-DAMES, and encamped.	
BOIS-DES-DAMES	8/8/18		Section in camp. Routine work.	
"	9/8/18		Eight horses & two mules evacuated to No XIII VETERINARY EVACUATING STATION.	
"	10/8/18		Six horses & one mule evacuated to No VII VETERINARY EVACUATING STATION.	
"	11/8/18		In camp. Routine work.	
"	12/8/18		One horse & one mule to butchers.	
"	13/8/18		In camp. Routine work.	
"	14/8/18		Ten horses & three mules to No VIII VETERINARY EVACUATING STATION.	

Army Form C. 2118.

WAR DIARY
or
INTELLIGENCE SUMMARY.
(Erase heading not required.)

SHEET 2.

MOBILE VETERINARY SECTION.
No. 31st
Date 1.9.18

Place	Date	Hour	Summary of Events and Information	Remarks and references to Appendices
BOIS-DES DAMES	15/8/18		Marched horses & two miles to No XII Veterinary Evacuating Station.	
"	16/8/18		Routine work. In camp.	
"	17/8/18		Six horses & one mule to No VIII Veterinary Evacuating Station. CAPTAIN J.A. DIXON. A.V.C. joined Section from A/87 Bde. R.F.A. No 15338 PTE. MAULE A. 3rd WORCESTER REGT. returned to unit.	
"	18/8/18		In camp. Routine work.	
"	19/8/18		In camp. Routine work.	
"	20/8/18		Three horses & two mules evacuated to No VIII Veterinary Evacuating Station	
"	21/8/18		In camp. Routine work.	
"	22/8/18		In camp. Routine work.	
"	23/8/18		In camp. Routine work.	
"	24/8/18		Section moved at 11 a.m. to billets at LAPUGNOY. D.19.a.9.5. (Sheet 44.B)	
LAPUGNOY	25/8/18		Section in billets.	
"	26/8/18		Two horses & one mule to No VIII Veterinary Evacuating Station. One horse to butchers.	
"	27/8/18		Section in billets. Routine work.	
"	28/8/18		One mule to butchers	
"	29/8/18		One horse to No XIII Veterinary Evacuating Station	
"	30/8/18		Five horses & three mules to No XIII Veterinary Evacuating Station. Evidently sick etc	
"	31/8/18		In camp. Routine work.	

96/10

WAR DIARY or INTELLIGENCE SUMMARY   Army Form C. 2118.

31 M.V. Vet: See Sheet 1

Vol 38

(Erase heading not required.)

Instructions regarding War Diaries and Intelligence Summaries are contained in F.S. Regs., Part II. and the Staff Manual respectively. Title pages will be prepared in manuscript.

Place	Date	Hour	Summary of Events and Information	Remarks and references to Appendices
LAPUGNOY Bg.D.q.s. (Enqueques)	1/9/18		Section in Billets. No T3/034357 DVR. BOURNE. E.C. A.S.C. attached 31st M.V.S. proceeded to U.K. for 14 days leave.	
"	2/9/18		Two horses evacuated to No XIII VETERINARY EVACUATING STATION.	
"	3/9/18		Two horses evacuated to No XIII VETERINARY EVACUATING STATION. Section moved at 2pm to LE HANEL (V.22.a.4.5) Sheet 36A. Arriving at 5pm. No 31096 Pte LUNN. W. 8th Gloucester Regt. and No 200471 Pte GROVES. B.G. 14th S.L.I. Regt. joined section for temporary duty	
LE HANEL (V.22.a.4.5) (Sheet 36A)	4/9/18		Section in Billets. Routine Work	
"	5/9/18		Eight horses & one mule evacuated to No XIII VETERINARY EVACUATING STATION.	
"	6/9/18		Pte CLARKE. S. 9th R.W.F. Regt. joined section for temporary duty.	
"	7/9/18		Section in Billets. Routine work	
"	8/9/18		Eleven horses & two mules evacuated to No XIII VETERINARY EVACUATING STATION.	
"	9/9/18		One horse to hospital.	
"	10/9/18		Section in billets. Routine work	
"	11/9/18		Section in billets. Routine work	
"	12/9/18		Section in billets. Routine work	
"	13/9/18		No 438944 Sapper OKE. A.P. B.S. FIELD COY R.E. returned to this unit	

A5834 Wt.W4973/M687 750,000 8/16 D.D.&L. Ltd. Forms/C.2118/13.

Army Form C. 2118.

WAR DIARY
or
INTELLIGENCE SUMMARY.
(Erase heading not required.)

Sheet. 2

Place	Date	Hour	Summary of Events and Information	Remarks and references to Appendices
LE HAMEL (V.22.a.u.5) (Sht 36A)	14/9/18		Seven horses and two mules evacuated to No XIII VETERINARY EVACUATING STATION. Captain S.S.KERR A.V.C. took command of Section. No T4/161157 Dvr KEANE A.S.C. and No T2/14169 Dvr. GREENSLADE. A. A.S.C. joined Section from 157 Coy A.S.C. 19th DIV. TRAIN returned to D.C.	
"	15/9/18		No T.T.03720 PTE ABBOTT A.E. A.V.C. admitted into hospital sick then 59th FIELD AMB. Captain A.R. SMYTHE. A.V.C. proceeded on leave to U.K. 15/9/18 - 14/10/18.	
"	16/9/18		Seven horses evacuated to No XIII VETERINARY EVACUATING STATION	
"	17/9/18		Section moved at 2.30pm to BELZAGE FARM W.22 d.6.8. arriving at 5pm No 26440 Pte. POWELL .G. 5th BATTN. SOUTH WALES BORDERERS attached to Section for temporary duty.	
BELZAGE FARM. (W.22.d.6.8) (Sht36A)	18/9/18		No 627 Sgt. ROBSON.D.W. A.V.C. admitted to 59th FIELD AMB. sick. Twelve horses and one mule evacuated to No XIII VETERINARY EVACUATING STATION No T3/024357 Dvr. BOURNE .B. A.S.C. attached 3 S.M.V.S. reported returning off leave	
"	19/9/18		Fourteen horses evacuated to No XIII VETERINARY EVACUATING STATION	
"	20/9/18		On Billets. Routine work.	
"	21/9/18		Twelve horses evacuated to No 8 XIII VETERINARY EVACUATING STATION. No 62839 PTE SMITH. W. 19th M.G. Bn. joined Section for temporary duty. No 37538 PTE GOULDING. W. 9th ROYAL WELSH REGT. joined Section for temporary duty.	

Army Form C. 2118.

WAR DIARY
or
INTELLIGENCE SUMMARY.
(Erase heading not required.)

Sheet 3.

Instructions regarding War Diaries and Intelligence Summaries are contained in F. S. Regs., Part II. and the Staff Manual respectively. Title pages will be prepared in manuscript.

Place	Date	Hour	Summary of Events and Information	Remarks and references to Appendices
BELZAC-E FARM. (M.22.d.6.8) Sheet 30A)	22/9/18		In billets. Routine work.	
"	23/9/18		Four horses and four mules evacuated to No VIII VETERINARY EVACUATING STATION.	
"	24/9/18		In billets. Routine work.	
"	25/9/18		In billets. Routine work.	
"	26/9/18		Six horses and two mules evacuated to No VIII VETERINARY EVACUATING STATION.	
"	27/9/18		Seven horses evacuated to No VIII VETERINARY EVACUATING STATION.	
"	28/9/18		In billets. Routine work.	
"	29/9/18		Sapper E. HENNEY No 126335 82ND FIELD COY. R.E. attached to section for temporary duty.	
"	30/9/18		No 26410 PTE. POWELL.G. 5TH BATTN. SOUTH WALES BORDERERS returned to his unit. No 3942 Pte TAMBLIN. B. A.V.C. reported from No 2 VETERINARY HOSPITAL for duty.	

31ST
MOBILE VETERINARY
SECTION
No....
Date 3/10/18

S.S. Kerr Capt. A.V.C.
O.C. 31st Mobile Veterinary Section.

WAR DIARY or INTELLIGENCE SUMMARY.

Army Form C. 2118.

31 Mot Vety SHEET 1

Place	Date	Hour	Summary of Events and Information	Remarks and references to Appendices
BELZAGE FARM W.22.d.68. (Sheet 36A)	1/10/18		Section moved at 0700 hours to PERNES arriving at 1200 hours. Six L.D.'s & one three horse limbs. handed over to 59th M.V.S. 7th Division	
PERNES	2/10/18		In billets at PERNES. Routine work.	
"	3/10/18		In billets at PERNES. No 63839 PTE. SMITH W. 19TH M.G. BATTN. returned to his unit for duty. No 18369 PTE. McGINLEY. 5/S.W.B.'s joined section for temporary duty.	
"	4/10/18		Section marched at 1630 hours to GIVENCHY-LE-NOBLE arriving at 1855 hours	
GIVENCHY LE NOBLE	5/10/18		Section marched at 0900 hours to SOMBRIN arriving at 1230 hours	
SOMBRIN	6/10/18		Section marched at 0900 hours to BOISLEUX arriving at 1630 hours.	
BOISLEUX	7/10/18		Section marched at 0830 hours to point between GRAINCOURT and CANAL DU NORD	
BETWEEN GRAINCOURT & CANAL DU NORD	8/10/18 9/10/18		No 27538 PTE. GOULDING. W. 9TH BATTN WELSH REGT. returned to his unit for duty No 607 SGT. ROBSON A.V.C. returned to duty from 230TH FIELD AMBULANCE, 74TH DIVISION REST STATION.	
"	10/10/18		No 6439 PTE. WHITFIELD. A.T. granted 14 days leave to UNITED KINGDOM from 12-10-18 to 26-10-18 Section moved at 1200 hours to NOYELLES-SUR-L'ESCAUT	
NOYELLES SUR L'ESCAUT	11/10/18		In billets. Routine work.	
"	12/10/18		No 72/1469 DVR. GREENSLADE. A. A.S.C. returned to No 157 COY. A.S.C.	
"	13/10/18		22 horses & 2 mules evacuated to No 17 VETY. EVACUATING STATION.	

Army Form C. 2118.

WAR DIARY
or
INTELLIGENCE SUMMARY.   SHEET 2
(Erase heading not required.)

Instructions regarding War Diaries and Intelligence Summaries are contained in F. S. Regs., Part II. and the Staff Manual respectively. Title pages will be prepared in manuscript.

Place	Date	Hour	Summary of Events and Information	Remarks and references to Appendices
NOYELLES SUR L'ESCAUT	14/10/18		Section moved at 1000 hours to CAMBRAI, RUE ST LADRE, arriving at 1200 hours	
			2 horses evacuated to 6 VETY EVACUATING STATION.	
CAMBRAI A.43.b.9.f	15/10/18		No 6582 PTE. GADORE. A.V.C. granted 14 days leave to UNITED KINGDOM. 19-10-18 to 2-11-18	
"	16/10/18		CAPTAIN A.R.SNYTHE AV.C. returned from leave to UNITED KINGDOM.	
			CAPTAIN S.S.KERR.AV.C. returned to No 157 COY. A.S.C. 17TH DIVISIONAL TRAIN.	
"	17/10/18		CAPTAIN J.A. DIXON proceeded to S.A. to VETERINARY HOSPITAL for duty.	
"	18/10/18		Section marched at 9.00 hours to C.W.b.5.9. Sheet 57b	
C.W.b.5.9 Sh.w.57b	19/10/18		15 horses evacuated to No 17 VETY EVACUATING STATION.	
"	20/10/18		13 horses & one mule evacuated to No 17 VETY. EVACUATING STATION.	
"	21/10/18		No T.T.03394 PTE. EARP. C. joined Section for duty from No 2 VETY HOSPITAL	
			13 horses & one mule evacuated to No 17 VETY. EVACUATING STATION.	
"	22/10/18		No 3992 PTE. TANBLIN. F. granted 14 days leave to UNITED KINGDOM. 24-10-18 to 7-11-18	
			Seven horses & six mules evacuated to No VII VETY EVACUATING STATION.	
"	23/10/18		5 horses & one mule evacuated to VII VETY EVACUATING STATION.	
			Section moved at 1425 hours to RIEUX arriving at 1530 hours	
RIEUX	24/10/18		Nine horses & two mules evacuated to 17TH VETY EVACUATING STATION	
"	25/10/18		Twelve horses & one mule evacuated to No 17 VETY EVACUATING STATION.	

Army Form C. 2118.

WAR DIARY
or
INTELLIGENCE SUMMARY.   SHEET 3.

(Erase heading not required.)

Instructions regarding War Diaries and Intelligence Summaries are contained in F. S. Regs., Part II. and the Staff Manual respectively. Title pages will be prepared in manuscript.

Place	Date	Hour	Summary of Events and Information	Remarks and references to Appendices
RIEUX	26/10/18		No 6518 PTE BOOTY F. A.V.C granted 14 days leave to UNITED KINGDOM 28-10-18 to 11-11-18.	
"	27/10/18		14 horses evacuated to 17 VETY. EVACUATING STATION.	
"	28/10/18		Three horses & one mule evacuated to No 17 VETY. EVACUATING STATION.	
"	29/10/18		10 horses and two mules evacuated to 17th VETY EVACUATING STATION.	
"	30/10/18		Routine work. No 6057 PTE TUGWELL R. granted 14 days leave to UNITED KINGDOM 31-10-18 to 14-11-18. Three horses & one mule evacuated to No 17 VETY. EVACUATING STATION.	
"	31/10/18		Two horses evacuated to 17 VETY. EVACUATING STATION.	

31st MOBILE VETERINARY SECTION.
No. ....
Date 5/11/18

A.J. [Signature] Capt. A.V.C.
O.C. 31st Mob. Vet. Section.

WAR DIARY or INTELLIGENCE SUMMARY

Army Form C. 2118.

31 Mot Vety Sec

SHEET 1

Place	Date	Hour	Summary of Events and Information	Remarks and references to Appendices
RIEUX	1/11/18		Section in Billets. No 6458 Corporal Dairey F. granted 14 days leave to U.K. 2/11/18 to 16/11/18	
"	2/11/18		" Two horses evacuated to No 14 VETERINARY EVACUATING STATION	
"	3/11/18		" Section marched at 0900 hours to ST. AUBERT. No 13365 SAPPER HENNEY returned to 82ND FIELD COY. R.E. for duty. No 10394 DVR. DOVE. 82ND FIELD COY. R.E. joined section for duty	
ST. AUBERT	4/11/18		No 634 SGT. ROBSON. D.W. A.V.C. reports sick, and was evacuated to C.C.S.	
VENDEGIES	5/11/18		Section marched at 0900 hours to VENDEGIES-SUR-L'ESCAILLON.	
SEPMERIES	6/11/18		Section marched at 1300 hours to SEPMERIES. Two animals evacuated to VILLERS. Nobby	
			PTE. FACEY. W. granted 14 days leave to U.K 8/11/18 to 22/11/18. Section moved at 1130 hours to JENLAIN	
JENLAIN	7/11/18		Sixteen horses and two mules evacuated to 14th V.E.S. No 244683 SAPPER WATERHOUSE. F. joined section for temporary duty from 94th FIELD COY. R.E.	
JENLAIN	8/11/18		Section moves at 0900 hours to BRY, moving again at 1330 hours to FLAMENGERIES. No 6583 PTE. MOORE. R. returned from leave to U.K.	
FLAMENGERIES	9/11/18		Section in billets. Seven horses and 3 mules evacuated to 14TH V.E.S.	
FLAMENGERIES	10/11/18		Section moved at 0900 hours to BRY.	
BRY	11/11/18		Section in billets. Eighty horses and three mules evacuated to No 14 V.E.S. No 3201 S.H. SMITH. HERRON. C.A. granted 14 days leave to U.K. 13-11-18 to 24-11-18.	
BRY	12/11/18		Routine Work.	
BRY	13/11/18		Two horses evacuated to No 14 V.E.S.	

Army Form C. 2118.

WAR DIARY
or
INTELLIGENCE SUMMARY.
(Erase heading not required.)

SHEET 2

Place	Date	Hour	Summary of Events and Information	Remarks and references to Appendices
BRY	14/10/18		Section moved at 0930 hours to VENDEGIES-SUR-ECAILLON. 4 horses and 1 mule evacuates to M.V.Ves	31st MOBILE VETERINARY SECTION. No. .... Date 4/12/18
VENDEGIES	15/10/18		Section moved at 0830 hours to RIEUX. N° 3992 D/M TAMBLIN. B. AVC returned from leave to U.K.	
RIEUX	16/10/18		Section in billets. Routine Work.	
"	17/10/18		" N° 6504 D/M TUGWELL. R. returned from leave to U.K.	
"	18/10/18		Routine Work.	
"	19/10/18		"	
"	20/10/18		"	
"	21/11/18		N° 6628 CORPORAL DARLEY. F. A.V.C. returned from leave to U.K.	
"	22/11/18		Two horses evacuated to N°14 V.H.S.	
			N° 18629 Pte McGINLEY. 5TH BATTN. SOUTH WALES BORDERERS returned to his unit for duty.	
			N° 6518 PTE. BOOTY. F. returned from leave to U.K. and hospital at MILITARY HOSPITAL, BRITTANIA BARRACKS. NORWICH.	
"	23/11/18		N° 454 SGT. WHITEHOUSE. J. A.V.C. reported for duty with Section from N° 18 VETERINARY HOSPITAL. N° 45895 PTE. NEWBURY. W. returned to his unit. 9TH BATTN. ROYAL WELSH REGT. for duty. Routine Work. N° 6514 PTE. FACEY. W. returned from leave to U.K.	
"	24/11/18		Section marched at 1045 hours to CAMBRAI.	
CAMBRAI	25/11/18		Section marched at 0800 hours to BUTTE DE WARLENCOURT.	
BUTTE DE WARLENCOURT	26/11/18		Section marched at two hours to CANDAS.	
CANDAS	27/11/18		Routine Work.	
"	28/11/18		Routine Work.	
"	30/11/18		Routine Work. N° 103914 DVR. DOVE. 82ND FIELD COY. R.E. returned to his unit.	

Army Form C. 2118.

WAR DIARY
or
INTELLIGENCE SUMMARY. of Captain A.G.Smythe. R.A.V.C.
O.C. 31st Mob. Vet. Section.

(Erase heading not required.)

Instructions regarding War Diaries and Intelligence Summaries are contained in F. S. Regs., Part II. and the Staff Manual respectively. Title pages will be prepared in manuscript.

Place	Date January	Hour	Summary of Events and Information	Remarks and references to Appendices
MONTRELET.	1	-	Routine Work, No. 448628. Dr. EVELEIGH.W.R. 81st FIELD. COY. R.E. attached 31st M.V.S. for Temporary duty.	
	2.	-	Routine Work, No. 787. PTE. HEATH. A.J. 31st M.V.S. returned on 2nd inst. from leave of absence to United Kingdom.	
	3.	-	No. 22579. PTE. BAKER. J.R. granted 14 days leave of absence to United Kingdom 3-1-19 to 17-1-19.	
			Routine Work, 10 horses + 1 mule evacuated to No 17 Vet. Evac. Station.	
	4.	-	Routine Work, No. 448628. Dr. EVELEIGH. W.R. 81st FIELD. COY. R.E. returned to his unit for duty.	
	5.	-	Routine Work.	
	6.	-	Routine Work, 17 horses + 2 mules evacuated to No. 17. Vet. Evac. Station.	
	7.	-	Routine Work, No. 8981. CORPORAL. LEWIN. C.J. reported for permanent duty from No 2 Vety. Hospital 31st M.V.S.	
	8.	-	Routine Work, 13 horses + 1 mule evacuated to No. 17. Vet. Evac. Station, MAJOR. FRANKLIN. B.A.D.V.S. attached for rations. 220 Labour Coy. MAJOR. FRANKLIN. B.A.D.V.S. attached for rations.	
			No. 12038 Dr. FITTON. T. R.F.A. + No. 22035 PTE. LUMBEY. from Divisional. Headquarters attached 31 M.V.S. for rations + Necessities.	
	9.	-	Routine Work.	
	10.	-	Routine Work.	
	11.	-	Routine Work.	
	12.	-	Routine Work.	
	13.	-	Routine Work, 12 horses evacuated to No 17 Vet. Evac. Station.	
	14.	-	Routine Work. No 752. SEARGEANT. WHITEHOUSE. J. 31st M.V.S. granted 14 days leave of absence to United Kingdom 137496-24-1-19.	
	15.	-	Routine Work.	
	16.	-	Routine Work.	
	17.	-	Routine Work, 22 horses evacuated to No 17 Vety. Evac. Station.	
	18.	-	Routine Work.	

Army Form C. 2118.

WAR DIARY
or
INTELLIGENCE SUMMARY of Captain A.R. Smyth L.A.V.C.
O.C. 31st Mbl. Vet. Section
(Erase heading not required.)

Instructions regarding War Diaries and Intelligence Summaries are contained in F.S. Regs., Part II. and the Staff Manual respectively. Title pages will be prepared in manuscript.

Place	Date January	Hour	Summary of Events and Information	Remarks and references to Appendices
MONTRELET.	19	—	Routine Work.	
	20	—	Routine Work, No 1907 PTE. BROWN.C. 31st M.V.S. granted 14 days leave of absence to United Kingdom 20-1-19 to 3-2-19	
	21	—	Routine Work, 12 horses + 5 mules evacuated to No 14 Vet. Evac. Station.	
	22	—	Routine Work, 8 horses evacuated to No 14 Vet. Evac. Station.	
	23	—	Routine Work.	
	24	—	Routine Work.	
	25	—	Routine Work, No 218411 PTE. GROVES. G. 4th H.S.I. attached 31st M.V.S. granted 1 months disengagement leave of absence to United Kingdom from 25-1-19 to 25-2-19	
	26	—	Routine Work.	
	27	—	Routine Work.	
	28	—	Routine Work, 13 horses + 5 mules evacuated to No 14. Vet. Evac. Station.	
	29	—	Routine Work, 6 horses evacuated to No 14. Vet. Evac. Station. No 52887 PTE. ANSTEY. R.A.? No 52078 PTE. LANFAIR. C. 8th GLOSTERS. No 26342 PTE. CRUTCHLEY.C. 10th WARWICKS. No 38716 PTE. M. ACE. F.H. 10 R. WARWICKS. No 66421. PTE. LUNNAN. A. + No 66367. PTE. DAVIES. W.S. 3d WORCESTERS. attached to 31st M.V.S. permanently for duty	
	30	—	Routine Work.	
	31	—	Routine Work, 25 horses evacuated to No 14 Vet. Evac. Station.	

A.R. Smyth
Captain L.A.V.C.
O.C. 31st Mbl. Vet. Section.